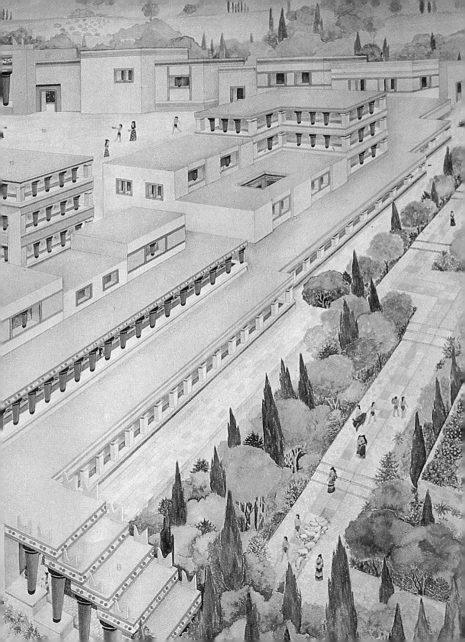

CONTENTS

THE BIRTH OF GREECE

Pierre Lévêque

DISCOVERIES

HARRY N. ABRAMS, INC., PUBLISHERS

Shortly after the arrival of the first Greek-speaking peoples, in about 2000 BC, a highly sophisticated civilization arose in mainland Greece. In time magnificent fortified palaces and rich tombs would bear witness to the new culture's development, which culminated during the reign of the kings of Mycenae in the 16th–14th centuries BC and ended with the invasion of the Dorians—another Greek-speaking tribe from the north—in the late 11th century BC.

CHAPTER I
A SUMPTUOUS AGE OF BRONZE

Strength and movement in a hero and a god: The celebrated Greek hero Heracles (opposite) and Zeus (right), the supreme Greek god, were given the task of reestablishing order in a world disrupted by the forces of chaos.

A knowledge of agriculture and animal husbandry had been introduced into this region around 6000 BC, brought by settlers from Asia Minor, where these skills had been perfected much earlier. It is clear that the indigenous peoples had been quick to adopt the new methods. Remains of settlements discovered on the fertile plains of Thessaly, in the northeastern part of the country, indicate the development of stable and well-organized communities. On the acropolis at the site of Dimini, for example, stood a true palace, indicating that even at this early date some monarchical institutions had already been established.

Homer's Achaeans— The First Greeks

Descendants of these early inhabitants had learned how to work with bronze only around 2600 BC, again somewhat later than the civilizations to the east. By this time they had obviously formed ties with the peoples of the eastern Mediterranean, for in their homeland there was no tin and only very little copper—the two chief elements used to make bronze. Subsequent advances in metallurgy and the manufacture of improved plowing implements and weapons served to revolutionize methods of agriculture and warfare.

The remains of a city dating from the Early Bronze Age (2600–2000 BC) have been excavated at Lerna, on the Gulf of Argolis in the eastern Peloponnese, the peninsula that extends its fingers down into the Aegean Sea. This was a region of active commerce, and according to legend it was at Lerna that Heracles would slay the Hydra, the

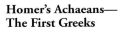

Some bronze weapons, such as the Mycenaean lance tip and sword at left, were utilitarian; others, like the one above, a double-headed Cretan ax, were highly decorated and designed for ceremonial use only.

monster with one hundred heads. Though the houses are still prehistoric in form, the presence of a fortifying wall attests to the community's need to protect itself against its neighbors. In the city center, dominating the whole complex, stood a royal palace known as the House of Tiles.

As yet there was nothing specifically Hellenic, or Greek, about this Early Bronze Age culture. The first true Greeks appeared only early in the second millennium BC, at the beginning of the Middle Bronze Age. They were a Greek-speaking branch of the Indo-Europeans, a race that originally occupied the vast plain stretching from the Carpathian Mountains in eastern Europe to the Ural Mountains, which lie to the east of the Caspian Sea. Other Indo-

On the fertile plains of Thessaly, in central Greece, archaeologists have discovered important human settlements from the beginning of the Neolithic period. The circular tomb below was unearthed on the site of a strongly fortified palace at Dimini.

European peoples eventually settled practically all of Europe and part of Asia.

The arrival of these new Greeks was anything but peaceful. The existing palaces, evidence of strong central organization, were destroyed. It would take centuries for Greece to emerge from the foreign and comparatively uncivilized conditions imposed upon it by the invaders. In the beginning, their tombs—unlike those of the indigenous princes—were not filled with lavish funerary gifts; their religion was more concerned with the relationships between the living and the gods than with the fate of human souls in the afterlife.

Homer, the renowned Greek epic poet of the 9th or 8th century BC, sometimes refers to these Greeks as "Argives" or "Danai," but his most common name for them is "Achaeans," a word whose origin is unknown but is now used to refer to this first group of Greek-speaking invaders from the north.

The only place unaffected by the Achaeans' arrival—initially, at least—was the large island of Crete, about seventy-five miles southeast of the mainland, which was inhabited by a highly advanced, non-Greek-speaking people.

The Palaces of the Cretan "Minoans"

Around 2000 BC, in an age of expanding population and increased production, the despotic rulers of Crete began to erect magnificent palaces for themselves. Within a few centuries, the island had been unified under the authority of the prince residing in the central palace at Knossos, a city on the north coast of the island. He was known as the *minos*. All of Crete's palaces were totally destroyed in the 16th century BC by an

Throne room and guard room (opposite, above and below) in the palace at Knossos. This priest-king with plumed crown (left) appears in one of the palace frescoes.

unknown catastrophe—perhaps the earthquakes and tidal waves that accompanied the eruption of the volcano on the island of Thera (modern-day Santorin), directly to the north. The palaces were immediately rebuilt, however, and in their new form they were larger and more magnificent than before. Their reconstruction attests to the great wealth and vitality of Cretan culture, then at the height of its power.

In the 15th century BC, however, the Cretans suffered both a new series of earthquakes that rocked the island and the incursion of the Achaeans. The Achaeans erroneously understood the term *minos* to be a proper name, and in later Greek legend "King Minos" figures as a symbol of wealth and power.

A storeroom at Knossos filled with large earthenware jars for foodstuffs.

Minoan vessels from the Cretan site of Mochlos (below).

Surviving frescoes from the earliest Cretan palaces portray the monarch of Knossos as a priest-king, but he was more than that; he was a god-king, one who demanded absolute obedience and devotion from his subjects. His august stature is commemorated in Greek myth, where it is said that King Minos was in the habit of conversing whenever he wished with Zeus, the ruler of the gods.

The palace of the *minos* not only housed the king, his family, and his numerous counselors, but was also the center of production in a carefully controlled economy. Its storehouses accommodated vast quantities of foodstuffs and other goods, and next to them were the workshops of artisans engaged in the creation of luxury goods for both domestic consumption and export. At the same time, the entire structure served as a kind of sanctuary and was imbued with a religious ambience.

The rulers of Crete were by no means as powerful as the Egyptian pharaohs or the kings of Mesopotamia, yet their authority was based on the same fundamental assumptions. The god-king was all-powerful; his

subjects, though not technically slaves, were absolutely dependent on him. A hierarchy of royal agents administered production and trade and saw to the division of labor among the exploited masses.

The mainstay of this powerful bureaucracy was a fraternity of professional scribes who kept detailed records in a script they alone could decipher.

In their overall organization, these Cretan monarchies appear to parallel most

This gold pendant (above) from an 19th- or 18th-century BC Cretan tomb is dominated by the imposing figure of the mother-goddess.

closely the small kingdoms of the eastern Mediterranean coast, which may in fact have served as models for them.

Labyrinths of Light and Color

The palace of the *minos* at Knossos was a vast complex of rooms and courtyards arranged on several levels. In fact, it is thought that the "labyrinth" that appears in the Greek legend of Theseus and the Minotaur was the sprawling palace itself. The structure incorporated flat

roofs and sophisticated hygiene facilities.

Everything was designed for convenience and comfort. The royal quarters were cool in summer and could be heated in winter by means of portable braziers. Even the smallest courtyard was bathed in sunlight and adorned with colorful frescoes. One of the most memorable fragments from these paintings is the female figure today popularly known as "La Parisienne," a highly individualized portrait with a noble face, large eyes, an impish mouth, and abundant hair.

Frescoes in a palace on the nearby island of Santorin reflect the same world of color and refinement.

Sea creatures are frequent motifs in vase painting and frescoes. Above: A 16th-century BC fresco of dolphins from Knossos.

Minoan frescoes portray individualized figures of great vitality. The girl at left is known as "La Parisienne."

Detail of a ceremonial procession from a Minoan fresco (below).

Amazingly well preserved, they depict blue monkeys, dark-skinned members of the royal guard, and boxers—all portrayed surrounded by a profusion of flowers, allusions to the Cretans' worship of a nature- or mother-goddess.

Cretan palaces were open and unfortified, for their builders were confident that Cretan fleets could repel any potential attack. Thanks to these same fleets the kings of Crete managed to extend their authority over the whole of the Aegean, creating a sea empire that the Greek historian Thucydides (460–401 BC) would describe centuries later. Their light ships traversed the entire eastern

Mediterranean, carrying Cretan vases and jewelry to mainland Greece, the Greek islands, Asia, and Egypt and returning with the mineral ores that were so crucial to their own economy.

The name Minoa—derived from *minos*—was given to Cretan settlements throughout the region, and evidence of the presence of these traders is provided by tablets inscribed in Cretan script. It is clear that Cretans enjoyed commercial ties with all of the Cyclades—the scattering of islands in the southern Aegean—and possibly with centers on the southern Peloponnese as well.

The "Cyclopean" Palaces of the Achaeans

In the meantime, on the mainland, invading waves of Greek-speaking peoples had imposed their rule over the native population. Their language appears on even the earliest surviving written tablets, from roughly 2000 BC. They established small, rural colonies that rapidly expanded, in part thanks to the influence of the Cretans, with whom they soon formed trading and diplomatic ties.

Perhaps their most imposing achievement was the construction of huge palaces, which their descendants —believing them to have been built by the Cyclopes, a race of giants—referred to as "Cyclopean." Probably the earliest of these palaces was the one erected in the 17th century BC by the Achaeans at Mycenae, a city in the northeastern Peloponnese, and continuously expanded in the centuries to follow. Its builders were the most powerful of the monarchs dominating southern Greece, and accordingly this era in Greece's history— corresponding with the Late Bronze Age—is known as the Mycenaean period.

This Mycenaean tablet (below) inscribed in the script known as Linear B comes from Knossos, and therefore dates from sometime after the conquest of Crete by the mainland Achaeans.

The animated hunting scene above—a masterpiece of Mycenaean damascening, or metal inlay work—suggests that there may still have been lions in Greece in the second millennium BC.

One of the as-yet-undeciphered Cretan documents is the famous Phaistos Disk (left), with pictographs neatly arranged in a spiral.

Unlike those of Crete, Mycenaean palaces had pitched roofs and were heavily fortified. Their walls were adorned with frescoes painted in the Minoan manner but celebrating the somewhat darker world of blood feuds and warfare memorialized in Greek mythology.

Cretan influence was evident in other arts, too. Mycenaean pottery, jewelry, and metalwork were produced using techniques that had been perfected by the Minoans. Just how the two cultures were related is very difficult to define, though it is clear that the

Mycenaean monarchs at one point owed allegiance to the Cretan *minos.* This has been confirmed by inscriptions found on many of the thousands of clay tablets that survive from this era.

The Work of the Scribes

Excavations at Knossos and at various Mycenaean-period sites have uncovered great quantities of archival tablets inscribed with unfamiliar scripts. The earliest of the Cretan tablets employed a system of hieroglyphs, known to archaeologists as Linear A, that has yet to be deciphered. Later documents from Crete and mainland Greece were written in an altogether different script, named Linear B, and it was not until 1952 that scholars finally determined that the language reflected in this script was an early form of Greek.

A massive arcaded gallery (opposite) formed a part of the palace unearthed at Tiryns, in the center of the region of Argolis.

The largest collection of Mycenaean texts comes from the archives of the palace at Pylos, including this tablet inscribed in Linear B.

In a sense these documents have been somewhat disappointing. They contain not a single reference to religion, mythology, or historical events, let alone early fragments of writings like the *Iliad* or the *Odyssey.* They are only lists of figures—mainly inventories and accounts.

But even this material can be helpful to the historian. For example, the tablets found in 1939 in the ruins of the Mycenaean-period palace of Nestor in Pylos, on the west coast of the Peloponnese, constitute a nearly complete set of records of the monarchy. There the king was known as the *wanax,* a mysterious term that is not

Greek and has no Indo-European cognates. The *wanax* was both a tyrant and a deity (there was a god of the same name) and organized and controlled the entire economy of his kingdom. In this he was assisted by a "leader of the people" (*lawagetas*)—apparently a position similar to a grand vizier or chamberlain—and a whole hierarchy of dignitaries, officers, and administrators who formed a bureaucracy like those of Minoan Crete or the empires of the Middle East. His kingdom was divided into provinces, each consisting of a number of rural communities under the authority of a chieftain (*basileus*). Now that so many of the

Linear B tablets have been translated, we can conclude that—contrary to what had previously been supposed—there was nothing feudal about the organization of the Mycenaean kingdoms; their institutions were those of a tributary state.

The tablets also tell us a great deal about agriculture in this period. Certain lands (termed the *temenos*) were owned by the king himself. Others were held by his retainers, and the revenues from these lands constituted their sole remuneration for services rendered. Still other tracts were dedicated to the support of the priesthood, with portions set aside as sacred precincts for the gods and ceremonies connected with their worship. Finally, though private ownership of land was not unknown, the greater part of what remained was considered common land. This was periodically apportioned to heads of families by royal agents at an assembly called the *damo* (a word that in later Greek became *demos,* the people). The form of writing employed in the royal archives of Mycenae remained unchanged

A 16th-century BC priest-king wore this gold diadem to his tomb.

The palace at Mycenae was primarily a fortress, but it was also a religious site of some importance. A pair of lionesses flanking a sacred pillar adorns its famous Lion Gate. As symbols of the mother-goddess, they ensured the sanctity of the palace precinct.

for centuries. It registered whole syllables rather than individual letters, and betrays a relatively unsophisticated analysis of speech sounds. (The Semitic peoples along the eastern coast of the Mediterranean, by contrast, had developed several consonantal alphabets as early as the Middle Bronze Age, 2000 BC–1700 BC.) The scribes employed as keepers of records for these monarchies contributed greatly to the power of their employers; their meticulous notations, illegible to others, constituted an incomparable exploitational tool.

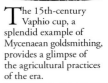

The 15th-century Vaphio cup, a splendid example of Mycenaean goldsmithing, provides a glimpse of the agricultural practices of the era.

The royal tombs of the acropolis at Mycenae were marked by stelae in flat relief. They were later enclosed in a circle of stonework, underscoring the sacredness of the spot where so many heroes were buried.

The Grandeur of the Palaces

Mycenaean-period palaces were also symbols of royal power—impregnable and forbidding. The earliest fortifications of the one at Mycenae were said to have been erected by the legendary founder of Mycenae, Perseus. They were repeatedly enlarged, but the remains of the earliest, dating from the 15th century BC, are still visible.

Over the course of the following two centuries were added huge ramparts securing the spur of the hill, a monumental entrance (the famous Lion Gate), and a back gate. In response to what appears to be a specific threat near the close of the 13th century BC, a hideout with concealed doors was added on the eastern side, and a tunnel dug to a deep spring, known as the Perseia.

The arrangement of the palace at Tiryns, a few miles to the southeast, was similar. There too a vast enclosing wall was added at the end of the 13th century BC, clearly designed as a refuge for people and animals in the event of an attack.

Common to the design of these mainland palaces was a central series of three chambers. First came two vestibules —one of them with an adjoining bathroom in which guests might wash and rest—and then a large hall, with four central columns supporting the roof. This great hall was known as the *megaron,* and though the origin of the term is unclear, the architecture of such halls, with their pitched roofs, skylights, and

Mycenaean death masks, which preserved the features of noted heroes in gold, the most precious of metals, reveal Egyptian influence.

fixed hearths, appears to have been developed in the North. The type seems to have made its first appearance in Anatolia (modern-day Turkey) rather than in Greece. Two adjacent great halls have been excavated at Tiryns. The hall at the unfortified palace at Pylos is decorated with a superb fresco depicting a young god of music.

The Wealth of the Tombs

Princely tombs became increasingly ornate in the Mycenaean period. The older ones are shaped like a shallow well or cistern and lined with stone slabs, while later ones consist of a shaft closed with a slab, or stela, sculpted in flat relief. Two circles of royal tombs unearthed from the acropolis at Mycenae are

of the latter type. The lower circle, which is slightly older, is covered over by the upper circle, which was enclosed within the walls as a sacred site. Both were sumptuously furnished, as though in illustration of the Homeric epithet "Mycenae, rich in gold." Still later tombs at this site were carved out of rock and provided with an entrance corridor. Of these, known as tholoi, or beehive tombs, the finest is the one called the Treasury of Atreus, believed to have been built in the 14th century BC.

Mycenaean palaces were veritable vaults for the protection of quantities of gold and jewels, the outward symbols of a monarch's prestige. The treasures discovered in them are characterized by a degree of refinement equal to that of Cretan work. Their quiet elegance belies the legendary violence and depravity of their owners. (The ruling family at Mycenae was the infamous accursed house of Atreus, including Agamemnon, Menelaus, Clytemnestra, Orestes, Electra, and Iphigenia, the principal figures of later Greek tragedy.)

Traders and Conquerors Opened Greece to the Outside World

The Egyptian pharaohs were well acquainted with the Achaeans—whom they called "the princes of the islands that lie in the Great Green Sea" (the Mediterranean)—and are known to have exchanged precious objects with them. The famous gold masks found in the tombs at Mycenae were once thought to have been of northern inspiration, but now it is agreed that they reflect the influence of Egyptian art.

Usually Mycenaean vases are ornamented with stylized designs; some, however, portray figures, such as those in the procession of warriors above.

The Hittites, who established a powerful empire in the heart of Anatolia (Turkey) in the Late Bronze Age, also knew these Greek peoples. In their texts they speak of the Akhkhiyawa ("the land of the Achaeans"), which may have been the Peloponnese or possibly a place closer to the coast of Asia Minor, perhaps the island of Rhodes. It is significant that the Hittite king appears to have treated the king of the Achaeans as an equal.

The Conquest of the Islands and the Coast of Asia

The Achaeans first tested their strength against the islands of the Aegean, their stepping-stones to the outside

In Mycenaean structures (such as the one shown opposite), doorways are often topped with corbeling, a common architectural solution before the invention of the arch.

Overleaf: A late 16th- or early 15th-century BC fresco from a palace on Thera (Santorin) depicts the departure of a naval expedition, an apt allusion to the Minoans' mastery of the sea. The palace itself appears in the background.

world. In the 15th century BC they even conquered Crete, the focal point of the eastern Mediterranean and, since 3000 BC, the center of a flourishing trade with the great empires of the East and peoples of even more distant lands.

In doing so, they helped to further Cretan influence, especially in religion, on the mainland. Mycenae became the intermediary between non-Greek Minoan Crete and the Greek city-states, the autonomous provinces established in the 10th century BC. Yet we know very little about the Greek presence in Crete; the archives at Knossos make it clear that an Achaean prince ruled there beginning in the 15th century, but the roughly three centuries of Mycenaean dominance over the island do not appear to have been an especially flourishing era. The western part of the island, previously underdeveloped, experienced a more rapid expansion, while the eastern part looked increasingly toward the Near East.

The Achaean invasion of Crete was a genuine military conquest, and it is quite probable that other such conquests lay behind the establishment of further outposts on the coast of Anatolia—among them Miletus and Colophon—and in Syria and Phoenicia by the 12th century BC. These regions bordered on the great Eastern empires, whose rulers could easily have repelled unwanted colonists. It is therefore possible that the eastern powers welcomed the presence of these outposts, considering them to be places of exchange and markets of benefit to both peoples.

As a symbol of extraordinary strength and courage, Heracles (opposite above) has provided inspiration for artists through the centuries. One of his labors is depicted in this 19th-century engraving (above).

Mercantile Expansion to the Edge of the Known World

The Achaeans conquered as much through commerce as through warfare. Mycenaean sailors undertook reconnaissance missions and regular trading voyages to the edges of the known world, far beyond the developed regions of the Egyptian, Mesopotamian, Hittite, and Luwian empires. (The Luwi were an ancient people living on the southern coast of Asia Minor.) Fragments of Mycenaean pottery found in Libya, Sicily, Sardinia, southern Italy, and even, discovered most recently, in the

The pitcher illustrated below is a typical example of Mycenaean pottery, which displays a remarkable uniformity in form and decoration. Here the main ornamental motif is the octopus, an element that is derived from Cretan art. Scholars have managed to establish a precise chronology of the period based on changes in the style of these pieces, and, accordingly, any pottery unearthed in the course of archaeological excavation can be used to date the site. This particular piece from the 15th century reveals the influence of Egyptian stoneware.

central Italian city of Florence, permit us to map their journeys.

Another indication of the extent of the Achaeans' commerce is the appearance of the name of the western Mediterranean island of Elba on tablets written in Linear B. Some ports—such as those in Sardinia and on the Gulf of Tarentum, under the heel of Italy—appear to have been so important that they must be considered permanent settlements, where regular trade in luxury goods flourished with the consent of local authorities.

It has been suggested that Mycenaean ships may have ventured as far as the coast of Gaul (present-day France) and the Iberian Peninsula, but apart from local imitations of Mycenaean pottery recently identified in southeastern Spain, no certain proof of this hypothesis has been found. In Libya, on the north coast of Africa, Mycenaean ceramics have been unearthed far inland.

It is quite certain that the Achaeans traded in Thrace, in northeastern Greece, and that they navigated the Hellespont (now known as the Dardanelles) and the

Bosporus, the straits linking the Aegean
to the Black Sea. There are abundant traces
of their presence on the western shore of
the latter, and by no means insignificant
ones on the east coast, in the region then
known as Colchis, where jewelry clearly
belonging to the Mycenaean tradition has
been discovered.

The Labors of Heracles

The Achaeans carried with
them not only jewelry, but also
foodstuffs, wine, and ores. They
returned with tin, an essential
component of bronze that could
be attained only in the East or
in Italy, the terminus of the
great western bronze trading
routes. The Achaeans also
coveted the fine trees they had
found in Lebanon and on the
Chalcidice Peninsula, in the
northwest corner of the Aegean.

These voyages are dimly remembered in Greek myth and legend, in the heroic sagas of Perseus, Bellerophon, Heracles, and Jason. Heracles, for example, was said to have already been a celebrated hero when his cousin Eurystheus, king of Mycenae, imposed on him the now-famous series of twelve labors. The first of these was to bring the king the hide of the Nemean lion, a fabulous beast living on nearby Mount Tretus. Subsequent labors took Heracles out into the middle of the ocean, to the mythical island of Erytheia—where he was to slay the monstrous, triple-bodied Geryon— and even as far as Africa, there to fetch the golden apples of the Hesperides, the daughters of Atlas. Clearly his was the saga of an early Achaean adventurer and conqueror.

Two vessels from the late 7th or early 6th century BC depict Achilles at the fountain (below) and Heracles confronting the triple-headed Geryon (opposite below).

Another early explorer is commemorated in the story of Jason and his Argonauts, who voyaged to Colchis, on the Black Sea, to recover the Golden Fleece and thereby guarantee the prosperity and power of the Achaean kingdoms. Jason never would have triumphed without the love of Medea, daughter of the king of Colchis.

In metaphor, these legends recall the enterprising early mariners who opened up new territories to Greek commerce. They are, moreover, splendid adventure stories filled with the romance of travel, passion, and miraculous exploits that have delighted generations of listeners for nearly three millennia.

Because of the enormous forces involved—and Homer's genius in narrating the event—the Trojan War inspired Greek artists for centuries. This relief fragment (drawing opposite above) depicts a series of major events from the conflict.

The Myth and Reality of the Trojan War

Another series of stories with a background in historical fact has to do with the Trojan War, fought in about 1200 BC. These tales were woven into the epics attributed to Homer—the *Iliad* and the *Odyssey*—some 500 years

later. There can be little doubt that the events Homer
describes actually did take place, especially since
archaeologists have unearthed at the site of Troy
—in northwest Asia Minor, south of the Dardanelles—
evidence of violent destruction dating to the very years in
question. Yet it is obvious that Homer's account includes
much that is pure fiction. Some authorities consider the
character of Helen to be a later addition and argue that
the Greeks' need to rescue her from her Trojan captivity
is a smokescreen meant to disguise an act of naked
aggression. In any case, the *Iliad* is as much a tale of love
and personal revenge as it is of military exploits, and we
can only speculate about the Greeks' real motives.

It has been suggested that Troy was of strategic
importance to the Achaeans as it dominated the land
route to markets to the east, a less hazardous passage than
the water route through the Dardanelles. Their real
interest was doubtless much simpler. Excavations have
revealed that the city was extraordinarily wealthy, owing
to its ties to the interior of northern
Anatolia—and thus with the Hittite
empire—and to various Mediterranean
ports. The Achaeans had no desire to
colonize Troy; they were interested solely
in plunder. Their destruction of the city
was so complete that the site was
subsequently uninhabited for centuries.
Whatever else it may have been, the
coalition of Achaean princes under
the leadership of Agamemnon was
above all a pillaging operation
against one of the richest cities of
the eastern Mediterranean.

There were other occasions when
the Achaeans banded together in the
pursuit of a common goal. Shortly
after their Trojan adventure, they
united to close off the Peloponnese
from the mainland by building a
massive wall across the Isthmus of
Corinth, the narrow stretch of land
connecting the Peloponnese with the

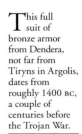

This full
suit of
bronze armor
from Dendera,
not far from
Tiryns in Argolis,
dates from
roughly 1400 BC,
a couple of
centuries before
the Trojan War.

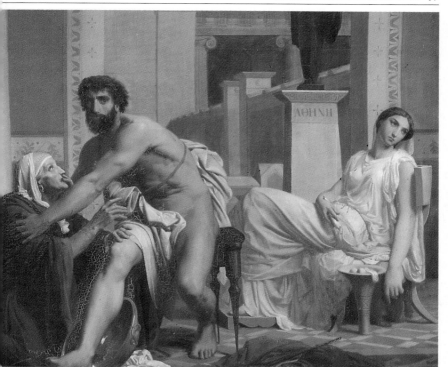

rest of mainland Greece. But they were never again as powerful as at the time of their siege of Troy, when they felt secure enough to be absent from their own kingdoms for years on end and wage war on the very border of the Hittite empire.

In this period the Greeks were truly masters of the sea, as is clear from Homer's *Odyssey,* a maritime epic detailing the adventures of Odysseus, king of Ithaca, on his homeward journey after the fall of Troy. For ten years he was swept from one end of the Mediterranean to the other, suffering shipwreck, falling under the spell of successive enchantresses, and finding himself obliged to navigate some of the most dangerous waters then known. At the end of the saga—a virtual catalogue of the perils and exotic creatures to be met with at sea—he

In this painting by Adolphe-William Bouguereau (1825–1905), Odysseus, having returned home incognito, is recognized by his old nurse.

arrives home in Ithaca to reclaim his kingdom and
rejoin his wife, Penelope.

According to Homer, Zeus and Hera Reigned Supreme over the World of Gods and Mortals

The gods mentioned in the Linear B tablets found on
Crete and in mainland Greece constitute a pantheon
similar to the one described by Homer and still revered
in the later city-states. With the exception of Apollo,
Leto, and Aphrodite, virtually all of the principal gods
were already represented, though not necessarily in
the same roles they would play later (Poseidon, for
example, is mentioned more frequently than Zeus). It
was a confusing assembly of major and minor deities,
which can only be explained as a blending of
Mycenaean and Cretan traditions.

On their migration into Greece, the Indo-European
settlers who came to be known as Achaeans, or Greeks,
had naturally brought their own gods with them. Theirs
was an extremely socialized religion, one perfectly
adapted to the need of these semi-nomadic peoples to group
together. It extolled the virtues of absolute authority,
military prowess, and fecundity, and in their various
ways its deities personified such qualities. The religion of
the indigenous peoples conquered by the Achaeans was
altogether different, featuring a variety of fertility cults
and a concern for the fate of the soul after death.

From the confrontation between these two belief systems
was synthesized a new religion that was apparently
serviceable enough then but is wholly illogical to us now.
Its many mother-goddesses are all derived from Crete,
whose Neolithic and Early Bronze Age cults had been
established to appease the hidden powers governing the
life force and to ensure the prosperity of flocks and herds
and the ripening of crops. This is made clear by the large
number of terra-cotta idols depicting the goddess of
nature, or the mother-goddess, that have been discovered
in Greek tombs. Following an important tradition dating
back to Neolithic times, she occasionally is accompanied
by a daughter goddess and her divine male child.

Cretan concern for the gods of the underworld gave
rise to cult practices that prefigure the elaborate mystery

An Archaic (8th–
6th centuries BC)
sculpture depicts the
union of Zeus and Hera,
the chief gods of the
Greek pantheon.

Enthroned on Mount
Olympus, an
impassive Zeus ignores
the entreaties of the sea-
goddess Thetis (opposite).
The painting is by Jean-
Auguste-Dominique
Ingres (1780–1867).

A religious ritual is preserved in this terra-cotta model of a shrine from Cyprus, an island in the eastern Mediterranean.

ceremonies developed on the mainland, the most famous of which were those associated with Dionysus, Demeter, and Persephone (or Kore) at Eleusis, a city located some fourteen miles northwest of Athens.

Significantly, the words "mystery" and "initiate" are part of the vocabulary of the Linear B tablets. Through initiation, one might be placed in touch with the forces of the underworld. The Greeks adopted and expanded upon these beliefs. In classical mythology, Zeus is said to have appointed as judges in the underworld three kings noted for their wisdom: Minos, Rhadamanthys, and Aeacus. It was they who decided whether the souls of the dead deserved eternal bliss in the Elysian Fields (a Cretan term) or were to be condemned to eternal torture in Tartarus (a region believed to be far below Hades).

Great princes were laid to rest in tombs elaborately furnished with treasures for use in the afterlife. It was believed that if properly buried and appeased with regular sacrifices they would continue to protect their subjects in death. In this way such figures became larger than life, the objects of local cult worship. In this context the tablets even speak of a "threefold hero," one whose powers are incalculable. From such beliefs it is but a short step to the all-important concept of the hero in the Greece of the city-states.

Omnipotent Goddesses

Though the Achaeans preserved some traces of their
own traditional religious thinking, they wholeheartedly
adopted the new deities they encountered in Crete.
In no time they were finding goddesses everywhere, as
personifications of natural phenomena, guarantors of

Bronze Age images of
the Great Goddess,
the source of all life, are
found throughout the
Mediterranean world. The
one pictured above dates
from roughly 1800 BC.

In this 15th-century BC
sculptural grouping
from the sanctuary of the
palace at Mycenae, the
goddesses Demeter and
Persephone take delight
in the divine child
playing on their knees.

fertility, and tutelary presences in this world and the next. The marriage of Zeus and Hera, at the summit of the Greek pantheon, is especially telling. It was a discordant union at best, to judge from the quarrels and wrangling we read of in mythology. And small wonder, for Zeus was Indo-European in origin—the supreme god, the god of thunder and of the bright sky to which he owed his name—while Hera was a goddess of the Mediterranean.

Later myths tell us strange tales about Zeus, revealing that his was a difficult birth, that his childhood was filled with danger, even that he died and was resurrected as a young god of nature. We even get a glimpse of him dancing as an adolescent in an attempt to summon the deepest powers of the earth. In these myths his relationship to Hera is highly contradictory; sometimes she is his sister, other times she is variously his mistress, his wife, or even his mother. None of this is surprising, once we recognize that the Greeks found it necessary to combine in a single deity the divine child—the imperiled offspring of so many Mediterranean goddesses—and the all-powerful, thunder-wielding father-god in the prime of life.

A Mycenaean bas-relief found in Syria (opposite left) depicts the goddess of fertility as mistress of the animal world.

Seal rings from Crete and Mycenae are often engraved with religious scenes. Here a procession of worshipers approaches the Great Goddess.

A model of a sanctuary is topped by horned animal heads (above).

The serpent-goddess below symbolizes the fertility of the earth.

The Collapse of the Palace Culture

The world of the Mycenaean palaces came to a sudden end about 1200 BC. The great unfortified complex at Pylos was the first to fall, soon to be followed by all the other palaces on the mainland and in Crete. Writing disappeared, as did the sophisticated art forms that characterized Mycenaean culture. In place of palaces were built only a scattering of more modest settlements. Why this occurred is a matter of continuing scholarly debate.

Four centuries of poverty and disorder known as the Dark Ages (roughly 1200–800 BC) followed the destruction of the palace culture. But gradually there arose a number of organized communities—the so-called Homeric kingdoms —and by the end of this period these had evolved into true cities. With them, the Greek world was ready to experience a second apogee, an era marked by colonial expansion and a wealth of creative advances.

CHAPTER II
THE ARCHAIC PERIOD: AN AGE OF SIMMERING CREATIVITY

Among the artistic marvels of the Archaic period are a scene showing women filling water jars at a fountain on an Attic hydria from the 6th century BC (opposite), and an exquisite bronze Apollo (right) from Piraeus, a city in eastern Greece.

The collapse of the palaces and the ordered society they represented may have been caused in part by earthquakes, in part by revolts by subjugated native peoples. Yet the main disruption appears to have been the immigration of the Dorians, a people whose homeland was in northern Greece, on the slopes of the Pindus Mountains. One by one the Dorians seized control of the wealthy Mycenaean kingdoms. It is possible to trace their movements by mapping the appearance of Dorian dialects in this period.

Theirs was not the only destructive migration during these centuries. In Anatolia, the Hittite empire was attacked and ultimately destroyed by invaders from the north, who plundered the entire eastern Mediterranean coast as far south as Egypt. Later historians referred to these invaders as the "Peoples of the Sea." On both sides of the Aegean, then, the established order was swept away, along with the tributary structures and forms of writing that sustained it.

Aeolians, Ionians, and Dorians Settled the Western Aegean Islands

A major movement of peoples followed these invasions, in the course of which the coast of Asia Minor (the

eastern shore of the Mediterranean) was settled by mainland Greeks: the north by Aeolians, the center by Ionians, and the south by Dorians.

The same distribution of populations can be seen in the smaller islands of the western Aegean and the larger ones close to the coast of Asia. Aeolians settled on Lesbos, Ionians on Chios and Samos, and Dorians on Rhodes. The latter were especially skilled navigators and managed to capitalize on the many opportunities for trade with the East that the new settlements presented.

Heavily armed and protected by his richly decorated shield, a hoplite, or foot soldier, from one of the city-states charges into battle (below left).

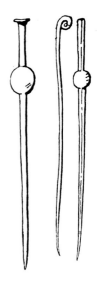

The forms of many utilitarian objects employed by the Greeks were adopted from the kingdoms to the east. The three pins above were used as garment fasteners.

The Rise of Homeric Kingdoms

Life in Greece at this time was generally brutal. It is likely that half of the population was decimated in the upheavals. The small communities that resurfaced, in many cases amid the ruins of former palaces, were primitive and isolated. They were made up of newcomers who had abandoned their semi-nomadic ways in favor of agriculture in permanent settlements. Each was ruled by a *basileus*, but these tribal kings were nothing like the all-powerful despots of former times. The new rulers were simply the offspring of tribal warlords who had led the migrations and claimed the best land for their people.

The king was assisted by a council composed of tribal leaders, men who dominated an assembly of the people

Magnificent bronze cauldrons like this example from Cyprus were produced in the Geometric period. They were used both in religious ceremonies and in daily life.

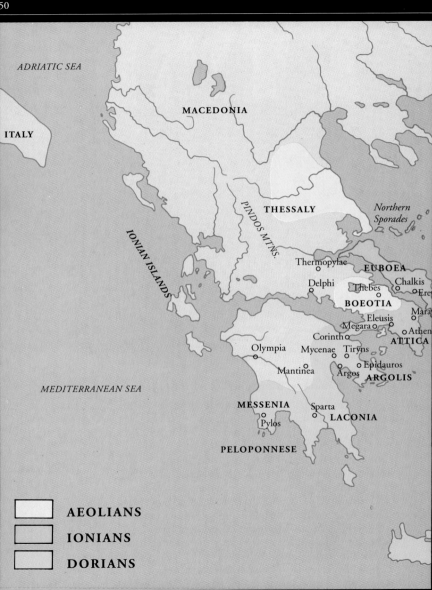

THRACE

BLACK SEA

PROPONTIS

HELLESPONT

o Troy

o Mytilene

Lesbos

Skyros

AEGEAN SEA

Chios

Smyrna   Sardis o

o Erythrae   Colophon
              o
              IONIA   **LYDIA**

Samos   o Ephesus

Delos   o Priene

Naxos   o Miletos

              Halikarnassos
Paros   o
        Kos
Amorgos
CYCLADES   Cnidus o

Thera (Santorini)

                        o Lindos

                  Rhodes

CRETE

o Knossos
o Phaistos

0   200 km

that had no decision-making powers. These were traditional Indo-European structures imported by the Dorians, and to some extent they prefigured the institutions of the later city-states. The new communities expanded rapidly, so that by the 10th and 9th centuries Greece was divided into a number of small monarchies, the kingdoms later described by Homer.

Many of the Cultural Innovations That Were Developed During This Period Would Have Far-reaching Consequences

Even during the Dark Ages, changes occurred that would help to shape later Greek culture. In the realm of pottery, for example, new forms were developed and a new style of decoration supplanted the old. First appearing in a version now known as proto-Geometric, the full-blown Geometric style would persist until the 7th century BC. Though it has been asserted that this was a Dorian innovation, it was in fact a product of native evolution, reflecting a new view of the world. The workshops that first produced wares in the new style were in fact located in regions that had not been overrun by Dorians, among them Attica, the region later dominated by Athens.

Equally important developments are apparent in the realm of religion. Increasingly, Zeus came to be seen as the one god with absolute sovereignty over the world of gods and people, a necessary symbol of authority in a time of insecurity. New deities originally from Asia were incorporated into the Greek pantheon and had claimed a permanent place in it by about 1000 BC. Aphrodite, goddess of love and beauty, for example, was a Semitic deity whom the Greeks first encountered on the eastern Mediterranean island of Cyprus; Apollo, god of sunlight, music, and prophecy, and his mother, Leto, were imported from Anatolia.

Amphorae in the Geometric style (example opposite below) were technically accomplished and richly decorated. Each of these two details (above and left) depicts a funeral; in one the bier is being transported on a horse-drawn cart.

The *Iliad* and the *Odyssey*

The Homeric epics were written around 750 BC, in the
era of the city-states. Yet they draw on a long oral tradition
established at least as early as the late Mycenaean age.
Homer himself could not imagine Greek conditions
some five hundred years before his time, in the period
in which the Trojan War was actually fought; at most
he could draw on his knowledge of the culture we
are describing here. His immense works, rooted in
history, are masterfully crafted, symphonic evocations
of ancient legend set against the background

Greece in the Victorian Era

In this painting by Alexandre-Louis Leloir (1843–84), Homer sings of the Trojan War to the accompaniment of the kithara, a lyre-like stringed instrument.

Following pages: *Greek Boy Staging a Cockfight* by Jean-Léon Gérôme (1824–1904) and *The Women at the Fountain* by Dominique-Louis Papety (1815–49).

ΚΑΛΛΙΡΟΟΣ ΝΗΙΔΕΣΙ

DOM. PAPETY
ROMA

of the so-called Homeric kingdoms. Poets like Homer were known as rhapsodes. They recited their works at the feasts of noblemen, singing of a glorious past and inspiring their listeners with the heroism of their ancestors.

The 8th Century BC Was Marked by the Rise of the *Polis,* or City-State, in Mainland Greece and Asia Minor

In time the power of the Homeric-era kings was diffused. Councils of aristocrats took over the administration of the kingdoms, annually electing one of their number as a magistrate. The people's assembly continued to be an important institution, one in which, by this time, even the poorest of citizens had a voice. Thus was born the political structure we now speak of as the city-state, an entity superbly capable of adapting to new military and commercial challenges.

In the typical city-state every person was accounted for and had a specific place in society. In accordance with Indo-European tradition, doubtless revived in the course of the Dorian immigration, the community was divided into various tribes, four in Ionian settlements, three in Dorian ones. Every individual was a member in turn of a family, phratry (clan), and tribe, and each of these associations was circumscribed by specific religious and political rights and obligations. Boys and girls were generally accepted into the community of adults at the age of puberty, in ancient rites of passage that were valued as a means of further solidifying the social fabric.

The Triumph of the New City-States

Archaeologists working in Greece have discovered iron artifacts that date from as early as the 11th century BC, yet it would be another two or three centuries before the new metal found widespread use. The appearance of much more efficient agricultural implements and

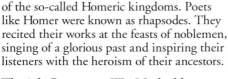

Left: Fine bronze weapons are still commonly found in Peloponnesian tombs from the 8th century BC, though by that time iron had become the metal most commonly used.

weapons contributed greatly to a sudden rise in population. Cultivation of the land took the place of cattle-rearing once and for all. More abundant harvests and over-production in other areas opened the possibility of trade—and increased the need for defense. The cities expanded rapidly, often through the joining of neighboring villages in a process known as *synoecism,* and the new growth served both to reinforce the institutions already in place and to stimulate a renewal of trading abroad. In the late Dark Ages (the end of the 9th century BC) a number of major Greek cities set about reestablishing commercial

The red-figured style of vase painting was a technique introduced at the end of the 6th century BC. Scenes painted in this manner frequently celebrate the lives of heroes. In the episode depicted above, the warrior Achilles bids farewell to his loved ones.

In this composition by French painter Jacques-Louis David (1748–1825), Homer elicits an emotional response from his audience.

exchange with the Near East and the peoples to the north and searching for new markets in Sicily and Italy.

Internal Developments

The city-states, ruled by groups of aristocrats, were not without tension. One of the earliest challenges to their authority resulted from the need of the newly wealthy city-states to maintain an adequate military force.

Heretofore the defense of these communities had been entrusted to these same aristocrats, the equestrian class, those capable of arming an effective cavalry force. But by the end of the 8th century BC there was no longer an adequate supply of horsemen, and it became necessary to enlist the services of the more prosperous peasants as well, arming them as hoplites, or foot soldiers. Inevitably, these new defenders of the city demanded new rights in exchange, not only an equal share in the booty of war but a greater voice in civic affairs as well.

A major agrarian crisis was another threat to the established order. In the countryside, small farmers found it increasingly difficult to survive on what they could produce on their own land. Since the custom of primogeniture, the eldest

In panels reminiscent of a comic strip, this bas-relief depicts young hoplites setting off to war.

A pair of running hoplites are portrayed here (below) in the black-figured technique of vase painting.

son's exclusive right of inheritance, was unknown to the Greeks, a farmer's lands would be divided up on his death among all his male children. It was not long before a given farmer's plot was so small that he could not afford to convert his wheat fields to vineyards or olive groves, for example, as he required an immediate harvest. He was also increasingly likely to incur debts to his more wealthy neighbors and ultimately—unable to repay them—to be forced to surrender his land. In Athens the indebted farmers came to be called *hektemoroi* ("sixth-part men"), as they frequently were obliged to surrender a sixth of their harvests toward the repayment of their debts. In extreme cases poor farmers were sold into slavery.

Temple pediments built in the late Archaic period were adorned with masterpieces of sculpture. This armored Heracles drawing his bow (below) comes from a temple on the island of Aegina, in the Saronic Gulf southwest of Athens.

By the 6th Century BC the Land Crisis Had Reached Such Dimensions—And the Gap Between Rich and Poor Become So Extreme—That Civil War Was a Universal Threat

The various city-states responded to this crisis in different ways. In some there was a complete redistribution of land. The response of Athens is credited to a single legislator, one of the first of the great Greek statesmen. In 594 BC, Solon (c. 630–c. 560 BC) became archon, or chief magistrate, of the city and was given

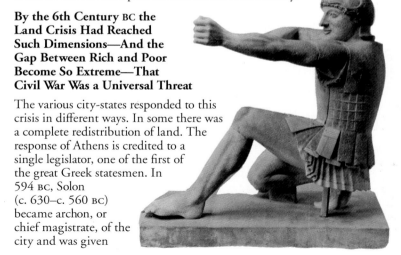

broad powers. He elected to cancel all debts secured by
land or the personal freedom of the debtor and to redeem
those who had been sold into slavery. He instituted
political reforms that gave the peasants certain political
rights and established the right of every citizen, whatever
his station, to seek justice through the courts.

In Corinth, a city-state located on the Peloponnese,
similar pressures had led to the establishment of a
dynasty of tyrants. Cypselus, who ruled from roughly
657 to 627, removed the ruling aristocracy from power and
gave its lands to his supporters, many of whom were
poor. As Solon would do in Athens, Cypselus reorganized
the city's citizens along tribal, anti-aristocratic lines,
and oversaw the establishment of a more uniform code of
law. His power, unlike Solon's, was absolute and passed
on his death to his son Periander (ruled c. 627–586 BC).

L etters from the
new alphabet are
found inscribed on all
types of stone.

The Birth of Democracy

In these states, as elsewhere, there was clearly a move
toward improving the rights of the people, the *demos*.
In Athens the change was especially rapid. In the late
6th century, Cleisthenes (c. 570–c. 507 BC) instituted
further changes in the spirit of Solon, reorganizing the
citizens into ten tribes so as to weaken the landowning
aristocracy. In so doing he paved the way for the
establishment of the earliest democracy.

A debate sparked by
Solon's plans for
reform is depicted in a
17th-century painting.

In other regions the move toward democracy was either much less swift or altogether stifled, and power remained in the hands of dictators or oligarchies. Sparta emphasized the equality of its freeborn male citizens, to be sure, but they constituted only a fraction of the populace. The majority was made up of slaves and helots, peasants dependent on the community as a whole. It was the latter who performed all agricultural labor, and they were treated with nothing but scorn by their citizen masters. More than likely they were descendants of the indigenous peoples who had been conquered by the Dorians.

The Greek Alphabet, a Recipe for Progress

At the end of the Dark Ages (about 800 BC), the Greeks developed a system of writing based on the consonantal alphabet of the Phoenicians. Theirs was an improvement, however, in that it also registered the sounds of vowels. With it, writing was no longer restricted to fraternities of professional scribes but was accessible to all.

The young poet Hesiod is inspired by a winged Muse in this painting by French symbolist Gustave Moreau (1826–98).

The results of this development may be seen in every facet of Greek culture. Laws could now be written down and consulted by anyone who wished to know his rights. Detailed commercial contracts could be carried from city to city. History and legend were no longer dependent on the memories of itinerant bards but could now be fixed in letters on stone or on any material one might write on. Philosophical and scientific speculation could be studied by all who knew how to read.

From Hesiod to Comedy

Among the first literary works to take written form were the epics of Homer. A near contemporary of Homer's—

and an equally shadowy figure—was the poet Hesiod, another early source of information on the world of the gods. But in his epic poem *Works and Days,* Hesiod also celebrated the lives of the obscure peasants of his native Boeotia, a region just north of Attica, offering notes on agriculture and navigation, praising honest toil, and espousing a moral life in harmony with both the gods and one's fellow mortals.

The 7th and 6th centuries BC are marked by a wealth of lyric poetry, smaller verse forms singing of love and passion, heroism, and death. Sappho and Alcaeus (both of whom flourished around 600 BC) were among the foremost early writers of such songs. Both lived in Mytilene, on Lesbos. Sappho wrote simple verses full of grace and melody, and she was widely admired and imitated. Alcaeus is remembered for his hymns, his political and drinking songs, and poems in celebration of love. Solon also wrote lyric verse, much of it intended to advance his ideas about the just rule of Athens. The poems of Theognis, from the late 6th century, extol the virtues of the waning aristocracy.

Tragedy and Comedy

The works of these poets were essentially personal, meant to be recited at intimate gatherings or read for one's private pleasure. Another type of lyric poetry—in celebration of heroes and the gods and expressing

The rapture expressed in this vase painting of a kithara player (below) suggests something of the Greeks' high regard for music.

the soul of an entire populace—came to be presented in choral recitations at major religious ceremonies, especially the festivals held in celebration of Dionysus, the god of wine.

It was from such heroic choral odes and cantatas that the new genre of tragedy evolved, in which one or more actors playing the parts of familiar figures from legend were set off against the chorus. The tragedies of Aeschylus (525–456 BC), Sophocles (c. 496–406 BC), and Euripides (c. 484–406 BC) are haunting meditations on the folly of unbridled passion and the abuse of power. Presented to the assembled populace as part of the Dionysiac festivities, they served to temper the behavior of the body politic and were powerful forces for the workings of the new democracy.

Comedy made its appearance slightly later. The first of the plays of Aristophanes (c. 450–c. 388 BC) dates from 427. These satirical farces were also potent weapons against the misuse of power and provided eloquent commentary on current events.

Greek actors performed in masks. The mask opposite would have been appropriate for tragedy, the grinning one above for comedy.

Metaphysics and Mathematics

A new spirit of rationalism becomes evident in the late 7th century. One of its earliest champions was Thales (c. 625–c. 547 BC), who was renowned as a statesman, astronomer, and mathematician. He was the first of the philosophers—known in their own time as *sophoi,* or sages—of Miletus, the southernmost city in Ionia, on the

This solemn religious procession advances to the sound of the flute and the kithara.

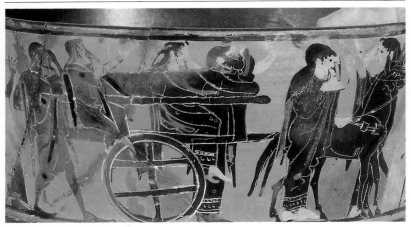

west coast of Asia Minor. Together with his younger contemporaries Anaximander (610–c. 547 BC) and Anaximenes (c. 600–528 BC), he sought to discover a *physis,* or underlying principle, governing the workings of the universe. Turning their backs on mythological explanations of the cosmos, these early philosophers based their speculations on their own direct experience bolstered by mathematics. There is no denying that they drew much of their thinking from the cultures of the East; however, their rational approach was wholly new and places them firmly in the philosophical tradition of the West.

Sixth-century philosopher and mathematician Pythagoras (c. 580–c. 500 BC) was born on the island of Samos but left it about 530 to escape its tyrant. He settled at Crotona, a Greek colony in southern Italy,

By comparing this funeral scene from a black-figured vase with those executed in the Geometric style on pp. 52–3, one can appreciate what profound changes occurred in the art of vase painting over the course of only a few centuries.

Considerable variation was possible within the various architectural styles. Below: A Doric and an Ionic capital.

where he founded a brilliant school of philosophy that combined a mystical sensibility and high moral purpose with a fascination with numbers as the keys to the universe. Pythagoras and his followers were the first to elevate mathematics to the rank of a science, and they contributed greatly to the early development of geometry. They were also among the first thinkers to conceive of the earth as a sphere.

This sullen maiden (or *korē*) is a masterpiece of the late Archaic period in Attica.

Religion and Politics

Religion was intimately bound up with the politics and economy of the city-states. Each had its own ancient civic cults, and each sought to outdo its neighbors in the construction of elaborate shrines to its gods. The best families, eager to add to their own prestige, frequently sponsored elaborate ceremonies in honor of their legendary ancestors. In time, however, the populace as a whole came to expect the state to organize religious observances—particularly those concerning Dionysus, Demeter, and Persephone—and in due course such demands were met. Tyrants, dependent as they were on the good will of the *demos,* were among the first to recognize the value of staging great public festivals for the entertainment of the citizenry.

Much of the new prosperity of the city-states went into the enlargement of temples and sacred shrines. Among the most elaborate sanctuaries were those at Olympia and Delphi, where Greeks of all races came together for periodic games and ceremonies of reconciliation. In an explosion of building activity, ever larger and more ornate temples were raised throughout the whole of Greece, and increasingly lavish gifts flowed into their treasuries. The superb structures of the Acropolis in

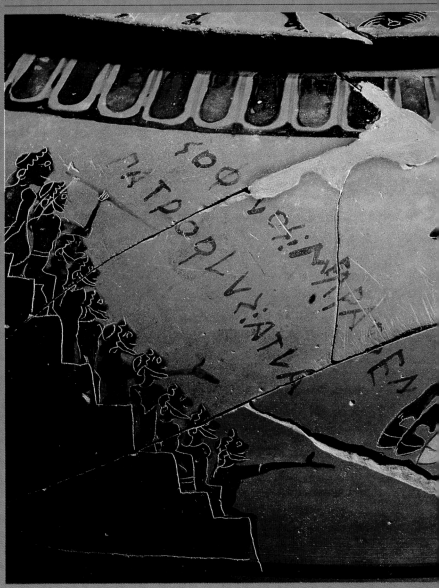

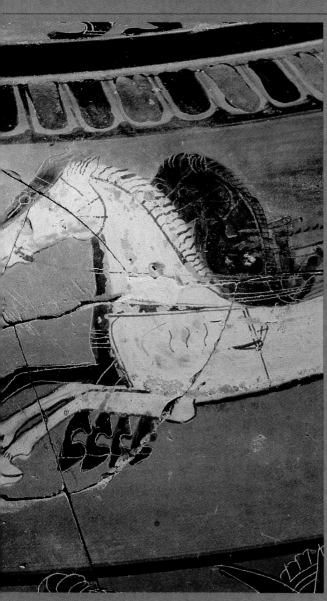

The Panhellenic Games

Athletic and equestrian competitions were staged in the sanctuaries where Greeks of all races convened and were a prominent feature of Greek culture. Artists frequently drew inspiration from them. This vase painting borrows details from the competitions for a depiction of the funeral games held in honor of Patroclus, as described in the *Iliad*.

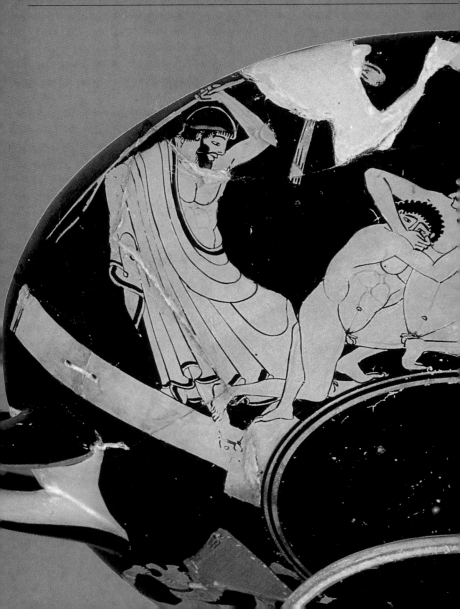

Gymnastics

Young men practiced wrestling in the *palaistra*—a public space devoted to the training of athletes—under the guidance of a gymnastics coach.

Athens, erected in the course of the 7th and 6th centuries, are only the best known of them.

The classical form of the Greek temple was derived in part from the architecture of Achaean palaces and in part from Egyptian and Eastern temple construction. Three distinct styles, or orders, were developed, each with its own specific proportions and ornamentation. The Parthenon at Athens (447–432) is a masterpiece of the Doric style, while the nearby Erechtheum (421–405) exemplifies the style known as Ionic. The latest and most ornate of the orders was the Corinthian, of which the Temple of Olympian Zeus in Athens (174 BC–AD 41) is a splendid example.

The Greeks' placement of columns on all four sides of their temples was unprecedented. Additional adornment was provided in the form of increasingly elaborate sculptured friezes and pediments. The architecture of the Greek temple would be imitated not only in Rome, but wherever builders wished to erect monuments of majesty and permanence—even into our own time.

Painters of pottery frequently incorporated ships in their designs— unsurprisingly in that they belonged to a seafaring culture. Warships were more streamlined than trading vessels, an example of which is pictured opposite. Many were outfitted with an iron ram at the prow for piercing enemy ships in battle, and some were powered by several tiers of oarsmen. There were two main models, the *triaconter* with thirty oarsmen (below) and the *penteconter* with fifty.

In the Last Years of the 9th Century BC, Greeks Everywhere Once Again Took to the Seas

Around 810 BC, groups of emigrants from the Cyclades and Euboea, an island northeast of Athens, settled at the mouth of the Orontes

River in northern Syria, at a site known as Al Mina, the ancient name of which is disputed. Greek products imported into this small community, including wines and oil and fine vases in the Geometric style, traveled up the river and on as far as Mesopotamia. Merchants exchanged these goods for fabrics, ivories, gold, and slaves, which they then sent to all the major Greek cities. Al Mina was but one of a number of such settlements, which were tolerated by the local kings because they stood to profit themselves from the increased trade. Soon the major city-states

Greek commerce was uniformly regulated. Here a merchant is obliged to weigh his merchandise in the presence of two official overseers.

were all engaged in exploiting new markets, following
the example of the Mycenaean mariners centuries before.
In a spirit of intense rivalry, they now looked not only to
the east and north, but increasingly to the west. The
culture of the Etruscans in Italy was highly advanced
and eager for Greek goods, even producing local
imitations of Greek vases. The first of the Greek
trading posts, or *emporia,* to be established in Italy
was on the island of Pithecusa (modern-day
Ischia) in the Bay of Naples, in about
750 BC.

Another important Greek venture was at
Naucratis, in Egypt, on the westernmost arm
of the Nile, which was officially recognized as a
concession by the Egyptian pharaoh in the
mid 6th century BC. These highly profitable
outposts had nothing to do with conquest
and resettlement; they were simply Greek
enclaves in foreign territories. But it would
not be long before they were followed by the
first true colonies.

After a Few Decades of Reconnaissance, a Rush of Colonization

Greek expansion at the beginning of the Archaic
period came about in much the same way as that
of the Mycenaean period long before. Major population
growth at home triggered the search for new markets

The landing of the
ancient Athenian
hero Theseus and
his companions is
depicted on a black-
figured vase.

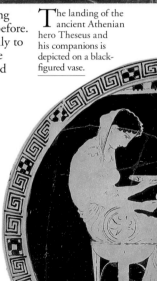

and opportunities for Greek settlement elsewhere in the Mediterranean region. Mainland Greece is mountainous and not especially hospitable to agriculture. It produced little timber, and its bedrock yielded only scarce amounts of copper and no tin.

In the scene to the left, a ruler consults the oracle of Apollo at Delphi. The priestess appears to be deep in contemplation as she listens for the voice of her god.

Even so, the arrival of the iron ax made it possible to clear its more marginal lands and plant them with vineyards and olive groves, and a dramatic expansion of the work force made it possible to achieve maximum production in such labor-intensive agricultural endeavors. Greece soon had a surplus of wine and oil, and these could be exported along with the metalwork, pottery, and textiles of its gifted artisans. The same population growth led to overcrowding, which was only in part relieved by reapportionment of land and the more enlightened policies of such statesmen as Solon. In some instances a city-state might simply exile a particularly troublesome sector of its populace. One such group was made up of the so-called *partheniai* ("sons of concubines"), said to be the offspring of helots who mated with Spartan women while their husbands were off fighting the First Messenian War in the late 8th century BC. Scorned in their homeland, they willingly left to find a new home, finally settling in Tarentum, on the southeast coast of Italy, in 707 BC.

Other colonists were individuals who, considered undesirable for one reason or another, joined forces to seek new lives abroad. Archias, for example, who founded Syracuse on the east coast of Sicily in 734 BC, had left his native Corinth because he was known to have committed a murder.

In a 19th-century engraving, colonists from Phocaea, in Ionia, have just landed on the site of what was to become Massalia. The daughter of the local Celtic king extends to a young Greek the cup that will make him her fiancé. Relations between native peoples and Greek colonists were not always so cordial.

The Oracle of Apollo at Delphi: A Priestess or a Powerful Political Tool?

People did not always leave their homeland of their own accord. When a famine struck Santorin in the early 630s BC, the powerful Delphic oracle (a priestess who served as a medium for the utterances of the gods) instructed Santorin's inhabitants to abandon the island and found a colony at Cyrene, on the north coast of Africa. The majority refused, and finally it was decided that those who were to emigrate should be chosen by the drawing of lots. Those who were selected were soon rewarded, for their new colony became extremely prosperous.

Above: A furious Heracles tries to snatch the tripod of Delphi away from his half brother Apollo.

The typical party of settlers set out under the leadership of a founder, or *oikiste,* and was forced to battle the native populace for land on which to establish a colony. They would first plant a bit of earth brought with them from their homeland, around which the new town was to be built. A surveyor in the party divided the new settlement into plots of equal size. The first structures to be raised were new homes for the gods, provisional temples generally situated on the highest bit of land, the *akropolis.*

The Greek Colony: An Independent City-State

Unlike European colonies in the modern era, these new Greek settlements were largely independent. Though in religious and other matters colonists might adhere to the practices of the mother city-state, and those of a given ethnic group might maintain close ties, they were free to steer their own political course. Any closer relationship with the founding cities was likely to be based on commercial interests. Miletus, for example, continued to dominate its colonies in the region of the Black Sea, and Syracuse, itself a colony, maintained control over its settlements on the Adriatic coast.

An early monumental sculpture from another temple at Selinus, in Sicily, depicts Heracles carrying off a pair of gnomes, the Cercopes, suspended from a pole balanced across his shoulders. These works, in a style inspired by the art of Ionia, were somewhat crude but extremely powerful. Later sculptures from the same temple complex (including the one on p. 79) display a considerable refinement and a highly dramatic sense of movement.

The majority of the Greek colonies are thought to have been established between 750 and 550 BC. First attempts at settlement on the Black Sea were frustrated by the native peoples of the region, and it was only the second wave of immigrants that managed to establish a foothold.

Colonists from Megara, a city-state about twenty-one miles west of Athens, settled a number of colonies in Thrace, especially along the north coast of the Propontis,

or the Sea of Marmara. Historically the most important of these was the one at Byzantium, dating from the second quarter of the 7th century BC.

The first colony to be founded in Italy was at Cumae, on the Bay of Naples, in 730 BC. But it was not long before the entire coastlines of southern Italy and Sicily were dotted with new Greek communities. One of the last major outposts to be established was Massalia, on the coast of Gaul (modern-day Marseilles, in France), which dates from c. 600 BC.

The colonial impulse was twofold, based partly on the Greeks' need for imported foodstuffs—especially grain—and various ores, and partly on their desire to open up new markets, particularly among the more cultured peoples of the Mediterranean. Some of these ventures were the result of spontaneous decisions on the part of individual cities or oppressed groups of people, yet there also appears to have been a degree of careful planning and organization behind the movement.

The oracle at the panhellenic shrine of Delphi played an active role in the whole process, urging emigration, granting religious sanction to specific groups of emigrants, and at times even determining just where they should settle. The sites selected offered either abundant fertile land for agriculture or maximum exposure to prospective buyers of Greek goods.

This head of a young woman is typical of works produced in the western colonies. Her hair has been rendered in great detail, and she wears the famous "Archaic smile."

A Westward Migration Following in the Footsteps of Heracles

Heracles, the mightiest of the Greek heroes, had journeyed homeward after his triumphs in Africa by way of Sicily and Italy, opening sea routes, founding cities, and siring offspring with countless local nymphs

The Labors of Heracles, as depicted in a 19th-century engraving.

and goddesses. The fact that he had been there long before seemed to justify to this later wave of eager merchants and colonists the use of force in snatching land from native peoples and reducing them to slavery; in doing so they were only recovering, as it were, their rightful inheritance.

Any number of city-states were responsible for launching new settlements in the West. Ionians from Euboea colonized the west coast of Italy and the Straits of Messina; Dorians from Megara and Corinth led the rush to Sicily; and Achaeans from the northern Peloponnese settled around the Gulf of Tarentum. The more prosperous of the new colonies soon spawned further colonial settlements of their own, thereby increasing their chances of continued success.

Social life centered on the banquet, whether enlivened with philosophical discussion as at Plato's *Symposium* or attended by heroes as at this one honoring Heracles.

Greece's Western Colonies Developed a Dynamic Culture of Their Own That Rivaled That of the Aegean Civilization

Prosperity came quickly to the new Mediterranean colonies. In no time they were building whole complexes of temples equally as large and splendid as those of Asia Minor. Those at Poseidonia (later named Paestum by the Romans, and now a small village called Pesto), on the Gulf of Salerno on Italy's west coast, and at Selinus, Segesta, and Acragas (now Agrigento) in Sicily still astound us today. Other public works such as theaters, marketplaces, and quays were constructed with equal opulence.

The western colonies produced a host of noted figures in literature, philosophy, and science. One of the earliest lyric poets of renown was Stesichorus (c. 632–c. 555 BC) who was born in Zancle (now Messina) on the north coast of Sicily, and settled in Himera, a nearby colony of that city. His retellings of the Trojan legends and the tragic matter of Thebes were celebrated throughout the Greek world and served as sources for the later tragedians.

Philosophy in the West followed in the Pythagorean tradition, with an emphasis on mysticism and moral conduct. Important representatives of this thinking are

The Temple of Concord is the jewel of the temple complex at Acragas, a cultural center of ancient Sicily.

Parmenides (born c. 515 BC) and his pupil Zeno (c. 495–430 BC) of Elea (now Velia), and Empedocles (c. 490–430 BC), who was born in Acragas.

In science, finally, no greater testimony to the high learning of the western Greek colonies is necessary than that it produced in Archimedes (c. 287–212 BC) the most outstanding mathematician, engineer, and physicist of the ancient world.

At the bottom of a drinking cup, Dionysus, god of wine, sails off on a ship surrounded by dolphins (left).

It is no exaggeration to speak of Greece's western colonies as a new world, a prosperous culture whose citizens lived comfortably, traveled, and freely indulged in the pleasures of life. Southern Italy was appropriately known as Magna Graecia, for it was in fact a "greater Greece" with unlimited new horizons.

Greek Expansion in the Region of the Black Sea

Greek foundations on the coast of the Black Sea were less glorious. The majority of the colonies in this region came later than those in the West, and they were founded in the face of much greater resistance from the indigenous peoples. They were for the most part outposts of the cities of Miletus, on Lesbos, and Megara, on the Isthmus of Corinth, and were concentrated on the north coast, near the mouths of the great rivers, the Dniester, the Dnieper, and the Don, which provided unparalleled access to the hinterland.

One of the most successful of these colonies was Olbia, near the confluence of the Dnieper and the Bug. Other tenacious settlements were established on the eastern

A modern engraving captures essential features of the cult of Cybele, the mother-goddess: Offerings of fruit are placed on an altar to the sound of rustic music.

shores of the Crimean Peninsula, near the rich fishing waters of Palus Maeotis (the Sea of Azov). On the eastern shore, three small colonies on the lowest slopes of the Caucasus enjoyed trading ties to the powerful kingdom of Chalcis, whose mines supplied mineral ores of all kinds.

Ores Were Important Commodities in Nearly All of the Black Sea Colonies

Various metals found their way to the west coast from the Balkans, and gold from as far away as Siberia was traded on the north coast. Foodstuffs were equal if not greater attractions. The sea and the many rivers flowing into it produced fish in abundance, and vast quantities of wheat were produced by the Scythians, people who dwelled in the steppes to the north.

The Black Sea colonies were less cultivated than those of the West, perhaps because they were in greater danger from vast movements of people in the hinterland, but they did play a crucial role in the economic balance of the great trading cities and the Greek world as a whole. They also produced certain remarkable figures.

Anacharsis, for example, a contemporary of Solon's, was a Scythian prince who traveled widely and visited Athens several times. He was celebrated for his wisdom

Cybele, seen here (opposite) playing a small hand drum, was a goddess the Greeks first encountered in their colonies in Asia. By the 6th century BC, she had been incorporated into the pantheon and a temple to her had been erected in the agora (marketplace) at Athens.

wherever he went and sometimes figures as one of the renowned Seven Wise Men of Greece (a subjective compilation that varies from source to source, but often also includes Solon, Thales, and Periander). Anacharsis was killed by his brother, the king of Thrace, for attempting to introduce into his homeland the Greek cult of Cybele, the mother-goddess.

This 5th-century BC princess wearing an elaborate headdress and an enigmatic smile was unearthed in Spain. She is a fine illustration of the fusion of Greek culture with that of the Iberians and Carthaginians in that region.

The Founding of Massalia in 600 BC Opened New Possibilities for Trade

Massalia, on the south coast of Gaul, became an extremely active port situated at the end of the great ore routes, especially that of tin ore from Brittany, in northwest France, and Cornwall, in southwest England. It exerted a strong influence on the entire Mediterranean coast and founded dependent colonies of its own further west. Among these were Antibes, near present-day Cannes; Arles, a few miles upriver from the mouth of the Rhône; and Agde, at the mouth of the Hérault River, about 120 miles to the west. On the northeast coast of the Iberian Peninsula—another region rich in desirable ores—Massalia established an outpost at Emporiae.

Colonization: A Two-Way Benefit

By the end of its period of colonization, Greece had access to the resources of three continents. In addition to the ores and grains it imported from Europe and Asia, it could count on a steady flow of gold, ivory, and slaves through its African outposts in Cyrene and Naucratis.

The tomb of a 5th-century Gaulish princess discovered in Vix, a town in northeastern France, serves to illustrate the benefits Greek trade brought to the so-called barbarians (in this case, Gallic Celts) as well as to the thriving culture of the Aegean. The princess was buried with the chariot that was to carry her to the next world. Around her head was a massive and quite magnificent gold torque, and lying next to her was a bronze krater, the largest and finest of Archaic Greek vases.

Her tomb, lying on the land route linking the Saône and Seine rivers, evokes the tin trade—the tolls exacted from the merchants of Massalia by the Celtic princes of Gaul and the diplomatic presents expected from them. It is a remarkable site, one that combines objects related to Celtic beliefs with wonderful Greek artifacts created at the opposite end of the Mediterranean Sea.

Another princess —this one Celtic— was discovered at Vix, in northeast France. For her pleasure in the afterlife she was provided with a beautiful bronze vase (below) and a solid gold torque (left), both of which had been gifts from Greek merchants. Such artifacts serve as symbols of the trade between the Greeks of Massalia and the interior of Gaul. Celtic objects were also placed in her tomb, among them the chariot that was to carry her to eternal bliss.

Greece developed its earliest form of democracy toward the end of the 6th century BC. Begun in the Athens of Cleisthenes, this progressive movement faced a formidable external threat in the attacks of Darius I (c. 550–486 BC) and Xerxes (c. 519–465 BC), the great kings of Persia, and an internal one in the chronic rivalry that developed among the Greek city-states.

CHAPTER III

THE CLASSICAL BALANCE: REALITY AND UTOPIANISM

Socrates (in a Pompeian fresco, opposite) introduced a new method of teaching that affected, in one way or another, all layers of society. The pupils at right are receiving instruction in music.

The Greeks had much contact with the Persians, and not only on the battlefield. The painter of the Darius Vase (left)—betraying a fascination for other cultures similar to that shown by Herodotus in his account of his travels—focused on the exotic costumes and furnishings of the Persian court. Another vase painter chose to picture a Greek and a Persian locked in combat (below), detailing the differences between their weapons.

The Army Dispatched Against the Greeks by Darius I in 490 BC Was Defeated at Marathon by the Athenians, But the Persian Wars Continued

A definite enmity between the Greeks and the Persians had existed since mythical antiquity, and by the end of the 6th century BC the territorial ambitions of the mighty Persian kings were bound to come into conflict with the Greeks' increasing demands for freedom and independence. Darius I had pursued a policy of conquest in Thrace, Scythia, and Macedonia and was determined to subject the southern regions of Greece as well. In 499

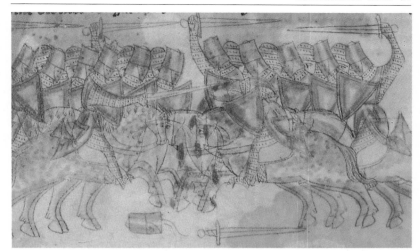

the Ionians under his overlordship staged a revolt, ultimately aided by forces from Athens and Eretria, a city some thirty miles to the north. The revolt was put down, but not before the Greeks had managed to burn the city of Sardis, the capital of Lydia, which had been captured by the Persians some fifty years earlier. Darius determined to take revenge. He instructed his majordomo to admonish him three times each day to "remember the Athenians."

The Persian fleet he sent to punish Eretria and Athens did manage to burn Eretria before its forces were stopped by the Athenians at Marathon, on the coast north of Athens. Still relatively intact, it then sailed away. Hearing of the defeat of his army, Darius was even more determined to conquer the Greeks, but he died before he was able to undertake another expedition. His son Xerxes finally set out in 481–80 BC with at least 100,000 men and over 1000 ships. On their march south toward Athens, his forces easily decimated the much smaller contingent of courageous Spartans who met them at Thermopylae, in central Greece. They then advanced against Athens and destroyed the city.

Under the leadership of the wily Themistocles (c. 524– c. 460 BC), the Athenians—joined by the forces of a

The battle of Marathon, which saw the Greeks victorious over the Persians, is the subject of this illumination from a 13th-century French manuscript. The two armies that clashed in 490 BC looked not at all like these groups of horsemen armed like medieval knights.

At Thermopylae, in 480 BC, a small contingent of Spartans managed to block the passage of the formidable Persian host. The painter Jacques-Louis David rendered this famous scene with great vigor and dignity. The Spartan hoplites, under the leadership of Leonidas, were prepared to die for their country. The sculptured bust above was probably meant to represent the Spartan commander.

number of other Greek cities—proceeded to confront the Persians at sea and won a decisive victory over the invader's navy at Salamis, a short distance to the west of Athens, in September of 480 BC. Xerxes retreated to Asia, leaving his cousin Mardonius in command of the Persian army. Mardonius and his troops were subsequently defeated at Plataea, thirty miles northwest of Athens, in the following year. The Greeks pursued the defeated army into Asia, driving the Persians out of Greek territory once and for all. Peace negotiations were opened, but it was not until thirty years later that a peace treaty, the Peace of Callias—named for the Athenian statesman who negotiated it—was finally signed.

The Athenian Empire

Capitalizing on their stature among the Greeks as a result of their successes at Marathon and Salamis, in 478 BC the Athenians promptly organized a defensive alliance with the newly liberated Greek city-states of Asia and the islands of the Aegean. The headquarters of this new federation was on the island of Delos, the site of a great sanctuary in honor of Apollo, who was believed to have

Most temples are adorned with scenes from mythology. On the temple of Athena Nike (goddess of victory) on the Acropolis, however, is depicted the historical battle between the Greeks and Persians at Plataea in 479 BC (below) during the Second Persian War.

been born there. Accordingly, the Athenian-led alliance was known as the Delian League. Its members swore an oath that they would remain united until the swords they threw into the sea resurfaced. For a brief time the league's treasury was housed on Delos, but in 454 the Athenians boldly removed it, placing it instead in the temple of Athena on the acropolis of their own city. This act of piracy was symptomatic of Athenian ambitions; in no time the city transformed what had been a voluntary confederation into an Athenian empire, brutally subjugating its allies, punishing potential defectors by the sword, and exacting harsh levies on its dependent states.

Though this small bronze (right) is only a copy of a famous work by Phidias, whose sculptures adorned the Parthenon, it exudes a power appropriate to Athena, divine patroness of the Athenians.

The Peloponnesian War

The larger and more prosperous
city-states bitterly resented
the usurpation of power by
the Athenians, and relations
within the new empire were
understandably tense. Sporadic
conflicts broke out, especially
with the great states of the
Peloponnese—notably Sparta,
Megara, and Aegina—until a
compromise peace was
concluded in 446 BC.

Athens was now
commander of the Aegean, a
position it maintained until 431
and the outbreak of a gigantic conflict
that would last for nearly thirty years,
the Peloponnesian War. The Athenians
imposed a series of cruel measures on the
cities of Megara and Corinth—positioned
at opposite ends of the Isthmus of Corinth
—whose economic interests threatened
their own. Sparta, the dominant city in
the southeast of the Peloponnese, chose to
come to Megara's and Corinth's defense
against Athens, whose arrogant
imperialism had become intolerable.

Two powerful blocks thus
confronted each other. On one side

Having formed the
Delian League as a
defense against Persia,
the Athenians established
its treasury (reconstruction
above) on Delos, the
presumed birthplace of
the divine twins Apollo
and Artemis. At that
time the island was noted
primarily for its religious
sanctuary, but it later saw
the rise of a wealthy
cosmopolitan city, the
center of all trade
between Ionia and Italy.

was the democratic city of Athens, bolstered by its fleet and the hold it had over its "allies." On the other were the aristocratically controlled cities of the Peloponnese, which relied heavily on their infantries of hoplites.

The first ten years of the conflict saw successes on both sides but no decisive victory, and in 421 BC the Peace of Nicias was negotiated, essentially restoring the balance of power that had existed at the beginning. But the treaty was soon broken by both sides. Then in 415 BC the Athenians foolishly responded to a request for help from Segesta, in Sicily, against its neighbors, hoping in the process to establish hegemony over the island. The Athenian fleet was defeated near Syracuse, and its troops either massacred or enslaved.

After that defeat, the Spartans were able to steadily gain ground until in 405 they managed to annihilate the Athenian fleet at Aegospotami, on the Dardanelles. Now, with the supply route from the Black Sea in its hands and Athenian communication with its allies cut off, Sparta could push for the surrender of Athens, which followed in 404. The once proud ruler of an empire was forced to hand over its ships and pull down its fortifications.

Battles elevated to the level of myth, like those of the *Iliad,* were a constant source of subject matter for artists. They evoke the clashes between cities that characterized Greek civilization, one in which war was endemic and peace never more than a temporary truce.

The End of Greek Independence Came in the 4th Century BC

It is relatively easy to understand the collision between Athens and Sparta in the late 5th century BC. They had long been rivals, even though they had joined forces to expel the Persians a few decades before. In the 4th

century BC, the situation became more complicated. The balance of power was constantly shifting as new alliances were concluded and dissolved. Once again the king of Persia intervened in Greek affairs, and Sparta's triumph was short-lived.

The Athenian expedition against Syracuse, in 415–413 BC, ended in disaster for Athens and marked the beginning of its decline. Captured Athenians were put to work in the large quarries (left) still to be seen at Syracuse, where most died of hunger, thirst, or their unsanitary living conditions.

Athens' strength lay in its navy, which was made up of light, swift ships propelled by three tiers of oarsmen. The city had several hundred such vessels all ready to leave port at a moment's notice. Below: A section of an Athenian bas-relief.

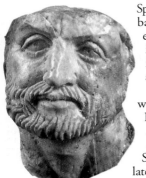

Sparta handled its advantage badly. Spartan conquerors established mighty garrisons in the beleaguered cities and in 386 BC concluded a shameful peace with Persia.

One of Sparta's subject cities was Thebes, the chief city of Boeotia, a region northwest of Athens. In 379 the Thebans managed to throw off the Spartan yoke and eight years later defeated the Spartans in battle at Leuctra, a few miles southwest of their city.

Though by no means as large as either Athens or Sparta, Thebes subjugated all of Boeotia and reigned supreme over the city-states of Greece after the battle of Leuctra, guided by the statesman and general Epaminondas (c. 410–362 BC). Under his command, Theban forces crossed over onto the Peloponnese on four occasions, attempting to liberate various of its cities from Spartan control.

Athens, meanwhile, had managed to recover from her earlier humiliation and to summon together a second confederation—this one with more autonomy for its individual members than that provided for by the Delian League of the previous century. Even Sparta was obliged to recognize the authority of this new alliance.

In 362 BC Epaminondas overwhelmed the united Spartans and Athenians at Mantinea, midway between Corinth and Sparta. While pursuing the fleeing enemy he was mortally wounded, and before dying commanded that the Thebans make peace with their foes.

Athens then regained the upper hand, but new blunders caused the defection of its allies in the second Delian League, and by 335 the city was so weakened that it was forced to accept a peace imposed on it by the Persian king Artaxerxes III (died 338 BC). Exhausted by over a century of war, it had no strength with which to combat the next threat to its independence in the person of Philip II of Macedon (382–336 BC). Craving peace at any

A gold comb found in a typical Scythian burial mound on the steppes north of the Black Sea shows a blend of Greek and Scythian art forms.

cost, it meekly submitted, first to Philip and, after his death, to his son Alexander the Great (356–323 BC).

Athens Versus Sparta

Writers on classical Greece traditionally focus on the dramatic contrast between the city-states of Athens and Sparta, but in doing so they mislead. In the 5th century BC, the period that saw the triumph of Greek culture, the western colonies were enjoying the peak of their prosperity. The arts of rhetoric and comedy were actually developed in Sicily, and that island's sanctuaries —especially those on the double acropolis at Selinus and at Acragas—were among the wealthiest and finest, most richly adorned in the entire Greek world.

Far to the northeast, a kingdom was created in 480 BC in the vicinity of the Straits of Kertch, connecting the Black Sea with the Sea of Azov, which produced Greco-Scythian metalwork of unparalleled artistry. Massalia, though less active in the 5th century, recovered its energy in the 4th century BC and founded still other colonies on the Provençal coast. The temptation to concentrate

The tomb of the kings of Macedon at Vergina contained a magnificent array of funerary objects. An ivory head (opposite above) probably represents Philip II, whose conquests changed the course of history in the Balkans and in Greece. The Nereid monument at Xanthus, in Lycia in Asia Minor, is one of the most famous monumental tombs of the 4th century BC. The war scenes on its friezes may be only symbolic, including this depiction of a city under siege (above).

solely on the exemplary antithesis of Athens and Sparta can be explained in large part as a surrender; the world of the Greek colonies is too rich and too diverse to be easily encompassed.

Athens and the Obstacles to Democracy

The power of Athens increased steadily from the time of Solon, the poet and legislator who first created a council drawn from an assembly of the people and courts that were accessible to all.

The tyrant Peisistratus (c. 605–527 BC), a relative of Solon's, widened the power base still further, and Cleisthenes (late 6th century BC), hoping to weaken the influence of the landowning aristocracy, divided the populace into ten tribes in place of four, and insisted on the right of every citizen to express his opinions (*isegoria*). He also improved the organization of the Council of Five Hundred and its ten divisions, or *prytaneis*.

Still, it was not until the middle of the 5th century BC that the reforms that brought Athens closest to true democracy were instituted, under the leadership of Pericles (c. 495–429 BC), beginning in c. 460. Pericles saw to it that most officeholders were paid for their work, so that even the poorest of citizens could consider accepting civil service appointments. Sailors, infantrymen, and cavalrymen also received payment.

Pericles wisely pursued vast public works projects, both to provide employment and to beautify the city. Thanks to the various types of payment for state service, the general populace attained a relative affluence, without which it could not have performed the duties

The potsherds above once served as ballots in determining whether or not a citizen was to be ostracized from the city.

required of democratic citizens.

The people's assembly (*ecclesia*) was the fundamental democratic institution. It was composed exclusively of free-born Athenian men; women and foreigners—even though their families may have lived in the city for generations—were ineligible. From the assembly a council (*boulē*) was chosen at random, and it was this council that appointed magistrates and supervised their activities.

The selection of members of the people's assembly to serve on the city council (*boulē*) was facilitated with this device (above).

Pericles, depicted below wearing his general's helmet, was in large part responsible for many of Athens' democratic institutions.

The assembly was composed of men who had no political training and were highly volatile; clever speakers could flatter them into voting against their best interests. Athenian democracy was thus exclusive and limited, but it was the most advanced political system in the Greek world. This was the first time that a people was permitted to chart its own destiny, accepting as its highest authority the will of the majority.

The workings of the *ecclesia* were in fact only as enlightened as those of its leaders, or demagogues. Pericles dominated it for nearly thirty years, wisely exhorting it to follow a consistent and constructive policy. His opponent Thucydides (c. 471–c. 400 BC) cynically maintained that the government of Athens was "in

appearance… a democracy; in reality, government by one man." After the death of Pericles there was no one as brilliant and clever to take his place; his successors were selfish and short-sighted orators. On two brief occasions, in 411 and 404 BC, the democratic constitution was even suspended after small groups of aristocrats seized power.

The Acts of Emancipation engraved in the sanctuary of Delphi (left) in the 4th century BC authorized a slave owner to grant freedom to his slaves if he wished. The Greek economy of the classical period was largely dependent on the exploitation of slave labor.

After Sparta's defeat of Athens at the end of the Peloponnesian War in 404 BC, the political situation in the city was highly unstable, and it is against this background of civil unrest that one must view the infamous trial of Socrates (c. 470–399 BC). The great thinker had served the state in war and in various civil offices, and had always upheld its democratic principles. Nevertheless, his outspoken manner had made him many enemies, and he was eventually accused of corrupting the youth of the city and failing to worship its gods. An obvious scapegoat, he was condemned to death and obediently drank the cup of hemlock that would end his life.

Following Sparta's demise in the 4th century BC, Athenian democracy revived. Payment to officeholders became even more widespread, and public service a respected way of life. Beginning in 400, a modest salary was even paid to citizens for their participation in the assembly. Yet in the course of the century there was a distinct waning of civic spirit, strongly condemned by the city's orators. The assembly began to dip into the theoric fund—a public appropriation established by Pericles for the purpose of financing public spectacles and providing for the poor—to pay for the army. Citizens increasingly resisted performing military service, forcing the city-state to rely more and more on mercenary forces.

In Contrast to Athens, Sparta Is Thought of as a Model of the Aristocratic Spirit— a View in Need of Qualification

The society of Sparta, the great city of the southeast Peloponnese, was quite different from that of Athens. It was divided between citizens, called *homoioi* (equals)— each of whom was allotted a plot of land by the state —and the virtual slaves who worked the land, known as helots. The latter were descended from the peoples who lived in the region before the Dorian invasion. Citizens were not permitted to undertake any productive work; they were all trained as soldiers, both to ensure their obedience to their leaders and to defend the state against attack. A third group, technically free but with no civil

Socrates, condemned to drink hemlock, a deadly poison, continues to converse with his disciples with his customary dignity (below). Though he left no writings of his own, Socrates was crucial to the development of Platonic idealism.

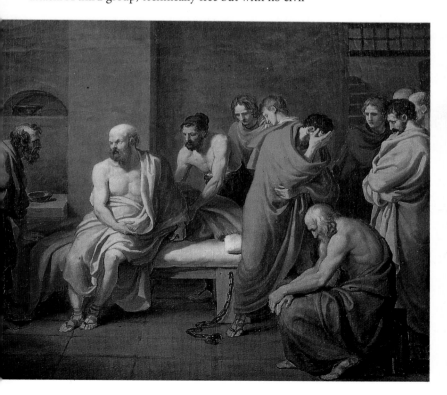

rights, were the *perioeci* (outside dwellers). They were permitted to engage in any occupation, including farming any land except that of the Eurotas River valley, which was called the "political land," or land of the citizens.

According to tradition, this social system had been established by Lycurgus in the 9th century BC so that every citizen would have an equal share of land to support himself and his family. As everywhere else, however, there was originally an aristocracy of citizens who also owned land outside the "political land." The influence of these aristocrats can be seen in the competitions held every four years at Olympia (the models for our own Olympic Games), where they monopolized many of the awards. So while the citizens of the city-state were technically equals, certain noble families could exert great influence. About 550 BC, an egalitarian reaction reduced the fortunes of the wealthiest of these aristocrats and prohibited them from trading abroad.

Redistribution of land in the interest of greater equality was not without problems. When a citizen died without

In this painting by Jacques-Louis David, Lycurgus presents the elders of Sparta with their new king. It is impossible to determine whether Lycurgus, traditionally credited with establishing the laws and institutions of Sparta, was a genuine historical figure or merely the stuff of legend. His notion of the city as a community of equals was soon discarded.

leaving a male heir, his property was awarded to his closest male relative, who was then obliged to marry the daughter of the deceased. Two or more parcels of land could thereby fall into the same hands, with no provision for any younger children. The citizens' purported equality was therefore a sham.

The system began to crumble in the 5th century BC. In 464 a group of rebellious helots took advantage of the panic following an earthquake and attempted to do away with their masters. Then, in 397, a conspiracy made up of helots, *perioeci,* and impoverished citizens rose up against the *homoioi,* only to be put down in a bloody defeat. Though ostensibly devoted to the institutions of the past, the Spartans passed a law at the beginning of the 4th century BC that permitted a citizen to mortgage his plot of land if not actually sell it.

With this law's enactment the Sparta of old was irrevocably changed. The traditional political bodies were preserved: a people's assembly, a senate consisting of thirty members, and an elected board of five *ephors,* or magistrates, that supervised the running of the state and the workings of the secret police. Boys continued to be given over into the care of the state at the age of seven and to be rigorously trained to endure all manner of hardship. But the old Spartan spirit had vanished, as various reform-minded rulers of the 3rd century BC would discover.

The legendary poets Musaeus and Linus, shown below, were credited with first combining recitation, music, and dance.

Athens Entered into the Glorious Period Known to the Ancients as the "Fifty Years"

The decades between the city's victories over the Persians (at Marathon, 490 BC; and at Salamis, 480 BC) and the beginning of the Peloponnesian War saw the triumph of Athenian culture and institutions. One result of the democratic system in Athens was the refinement of public speaking. The real founder of rhetoric as an art was Corax of Syracuse (c. 466 BC). It was Corax who demonstrated that one might persuade through reason no matter which side of an issue one argued. His teachings were further refined by his countryman and pupil Tisias.

In the late 5th and 4th centuries rhetoric attained its fullest flowering at the hands of the sophists, teachers of philosophy and oratory in Athens. Effective public speaking was required both in the law courts and in the people's assembly. If a defendant could not afford to hire a professional to plead his case, he might pay a speechwriter to produce a convincing argument for him to read himself.

One of the most successful orators to address the people's assembly was Demosthenes (384–322 BC), whose passionate harangues in the defense of the city against the encroachments of Philip II of Macedon are still models of

The two greatest thinkers of the 4th century BC were Plato and his pupil Aristotle. In his fresco *The School of Athens* (opposite) in the Vatican, Raphael (1483–1520) depicted the two in conversation.

Schoolmasters, or pedagogues, taught letters, arithmetic, and music. It is therefore not surprising that Greek citizens derived such pleasure from dramatic performances relying on a highly cultured audience.

reasoned pleading. Another forum for orators was provided by the assemblies at the Olympic competitions. The speechwriter and teacher Isocrates (436–338 BC) is most famous for the panegyric, or festival speech, he composed for the hundredth Olympiad in 380 BC.

The works of the great tragedians, Aeschylus, Sophocles, and Euripides, were also written during the "Fifty Years." Tragedy served to reinforce the spirit of democracy and drew inspiration from it. Taking as its subject matter the lives of legendary figures from the past, it was a highly effective instrument in the promulgation of the ideals of moderation and right conduct. By contrast, comedy concentrated on the present, poking fun at well-known figures and sparking debate on specific issues of the moment. Comedy made

Demosthenes (below) was a brilliant Athenian orator and statesman.

its appearance quite late in the period in question; its greatest practitioner, Aristophanes (c. 450–c. 388 BC), brought out his first play in 427 BC, after the beginning of the Peloponnesian War. For proof of the close links between tragedy and comedy and the exercise of democracy in Athens, one need only note how the two types of theater evolved in the following century. Tragedy declined along with the waning of a sense of civic responsibility, while comedy as conceived by Aristophanes —actually a kind of farcical review—gave way to the so-called New Comedy as represented by Menander (342–c. 291 BC). Menander's plays are not so much political parodies as escapist entertainments featuring domestic difficulties, mistaken identities, and the triumph of love.

The double bust at left portrays Herodotus and Thucydides, the founders of historical writing in a century so lucid that it could reflect on its own fate. A bust of Plato (opposite) glows with serenity. Philosophical discussion (below) helped to define democracy.

Herodotus and Thucydides: The Beginnings of History

Herodotus (c. 484–c. 425 BC), a native of Halicarnassus in Asia Minor, is called the "father of history" because he was the first to attempt to write a detailed account of a historical event. His primary subject was the conflict between Greeks and Persians that culminated in the Persian Wars (500–449 BC), but in the course of his narration he included a wealth of valuable information he had gleaned on his travels. After him, Thucydides (460–401 BC) chose to analyze the course of the Peloponnesian War (431–404 BC). His was a far more disciplined style of historical writing, with none of the charming digressions that Herodotus permitted himself. Thucydides was concerned to uncover the strict truth behind the events he narrated and constantly questioned his sources. His approach to history would have the greater influence on subsequent historians.

The Most Rational Pursuits—Mathematics and Philosophy—Played a Very Important Role

As we have seen, Greek philosophy began with the speculations of Thales in the 6th century BC. He was

the first to question mythological explanations of the physical world and to seek to discover its underlying principle through observation and logic. All of the early philosophers set themselves a similar goal. The sophists of 5th-century Athens—self-proclaimed teachers of philosophy—were less rigorous in their thinking, indulging in the pursuit of all knowledge for its own sake. In the person of Socrates, Greek philosophy took a new turn. A thoroughgoing skeptic, Socrates rejected the physical theories of the 6th-century thinkers as unprovable and scorned the sophists of his own century for presuming to possess superior knowledge that they might teach for payment. He likewise deprecated himself, refusing to call himself anything

This relief is one of the most moving works by the sculptor Phidias (5th century BC). Here we see the very origin of cereal cultivation, the moment at which—out of goodwill toward humankind—two goddesses, Demeter and Persephone, are about to give Triptolemus, revered as the inventor of agriculture, the first grains of wheat. With this gift humanity was placed on the path to civilization.

more than an "inquirer," one who engaged in informal discussions with his admirers for the sole purpose of inducing them to substitute good opinions—that is, opinions supportive of the common good—for bad ones, and to question their preconceptions.

Unlike Socrates, his pupil Plato (c. 428–c. 347 BC) developed a distinct system of thought, according to which the world of appearances is only a reflection of a superior realm of ideas. According to him one is elevated to an understanding of that ideal realm by beauty and love. In his writings Plato pays homage to his mentor, Socrates, and investigates everything

from the exalted influence of love to the proper governance of the state. Plato founded a school in the garden of an institution known as the Academy and taught there for forty years. His most famous pupil was Aristotle (384–322 BC), whose immense body of writings includes treatises on logic, natural science, metaphysics, moral philosophy, rhetoric, and poetics. He too founded a school outside the city of Athens, but only after he had first served for seven years as tutor to Alexander the Great.

Art Served to Elaborate on the Discourse Between the City and Its Gods

Artistic innovations of the 5th century BC tended toward the monumental and the decorative. The temple of Zeus at Olympia—begun in the previous century but only completed in the 450s— was adorned with fine architectural sculptures

On the pediment of the temple of Zeus at Olympia, a group of centaurs aroused by wine attack young women and adolescent boys at the wedding of the king of the Lapithae and Hippodamia. Here the bride herself is being abducted. Fortunately, a serene Apollo presides over the scene, and it is obvious that the centaurs will be obliged to retreat.

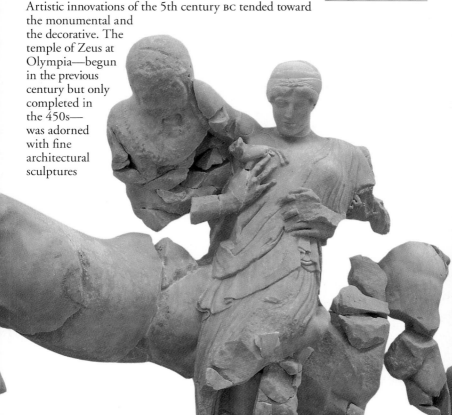

evoking a Heracles as pensive as he was energetic. The vast initiation hall in the sanctuary at Eleusis contained the masterpiece of the sculptor Phidias (c. 490–c. 430 BC), a bas-relief depicting the divine child Triptolemus receiving from the goddesses Demeter and Persephone the sacred grains of wheat from which all future harvests would grow.

The greatest artistic achievement of 5th-century Athens was the design and execution of the architectural complex of the Acropolis, which was initiated by Pericles and oversaw by Phidias. It brought together three temples to Athena within an enclosing wall in which ancient Mycenaean-period stonework is still visible. Leading up to the precinct is a monumental entrance, the

All of Athens participated in the Panathenaea, the annual festival in honor of the city's patron goddess. In one of its most important rituals, a procession threaded its way up to the Acropolis, carrying new ceremonial garments for the revered Athena.

Propylaea. Inside stood remnants of structures of great antiquity alongside new construction, most notably the glorious Parthenon, a kind of treasure-house for the Athenian state and temple to its divine patroness. Each of the new buildings was ornamented with exquisite sculptures, but those of the Parthenon were exceptionally rich. One of its pediments depicted the birth of Athena, the other her rivalry with her uncle, Poseidon. In the form of symbolic battles with centaurs (creatures fabled to be half man and half horse), Amazons (mythological female warriors), and giants, its metopes narrate the triumph of order over disorder. Finally, the continuous frieze adorning the top of the exterior walls presents a

On a frieze from the Parthenon, the sculptor Phidias depicted that procession, filled with a cross section of the citizenry of Athens moving forward to the solemn rhythms of religious music. The worshipers advance toward the temple's main facade, where they are received by a grouping of the gods at a banquet on Mt. Olympus (overleaf).

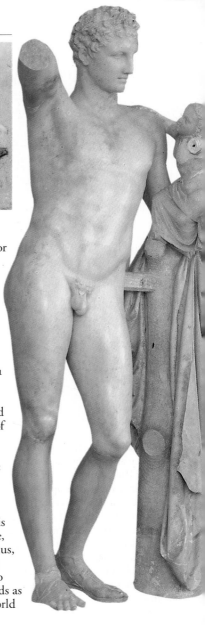

cross section of everyday Athenian life. In a magnificent procession representing that of the Panathenaea—an annual festival in honor of the goddess—horsemen, magistrates, maidens carrying on their heads baskets filled with offerings, and exotic residents of the city move forward toward the majestic grouping of the gods portrayed on the temple facade, benevolent but aloof from the world of humankind.

The art of the "Fifty Years" is majestic and serene, reflecting the self-confidence of a people triumphant on land and sea. By the end of the 5th century, after Athens had suffered defeat in the Peloponnesian War and its dominance had been broken, the works of its sculptors reveal a new restlessness; the earlier serenity is lost. Vase painting also reflects the change—it now employs a hectic polychromy.

Artists of the 4th century experimented increasingly with new forms. Among the notable new departures in architecture in this period was the elegant tholos, or round temple, erected in the sanctuary dedicated to Asclepius, the god of healing, at Epidaurus, on the east coast of the Peloponnese. Sculptors sought to give more life to the stone, to portray the gods as living beings, bringing them closer to the world of human suffering. Praxiteles (370–330 BC) sculpted slender youths and languishing maidens in such daring poses that they could barely stand upright, and a statue of Hermes carrying the infant Dionysus, the god destined to bring salvation to the world through love. The figures of Scopas, another 4th-century sculptor, are marked by strong emotion in their facial expressions and tortured movements. Lysippus (active c. 372–316 BC) created a new canon of ideal proportions for the human figure, making the head smaller and the legs longer. He is also famous for having been the favorite sculptor of Alexander the Great and the author of numerous portraits of the Macedonian conqueror. Common to all of the sculpture from this troubled period is an anxious unrest, a questioning fervor suggestive of a new impatience with the gods.

The Persian Wars Reinforced the Greeks' Faith in Their Gods, But Religion Was Also Assuming New Forms

In their triumph after driving the Persians out of their territories, the Greeks showed their gratitude to the gods

Seated gods (opposite left) on the frieze of the Parthenon. Hermes, in a statue by Praxiteles (opposite right), carries the infant Dionysus. A bust of Alexander the Great by Lysippus (below) radiates an inner energy. At bottom, a reconstruction of a tholos, or circular temple, at Epidaurus.

FAÇADE OVEST
RESTAVRATION

The Pride of Greece

Major groupings of Greek religious buildings continue to impress us with their grandeur, whether on the Acropolis at Athens or in the Panhellenic sanctuaries at Olympia and Delphi. After it was destroyed by the Persians, the Acropolis was rebuilt at the instigation of Pericles, who found an outstanding ally in the sculptor and architect Phidias.

On the following pages, a reconstruction of the Altis, the sacred enclosure at Olympia, and an imaginary cross section of the Parthenon, featuring the famous statue of Athena by Phidias.

AUTEL DE ZEUS

HIERON DE ZEUS

METROON

AGORA

ENTRÉE DES PROCESSIONS

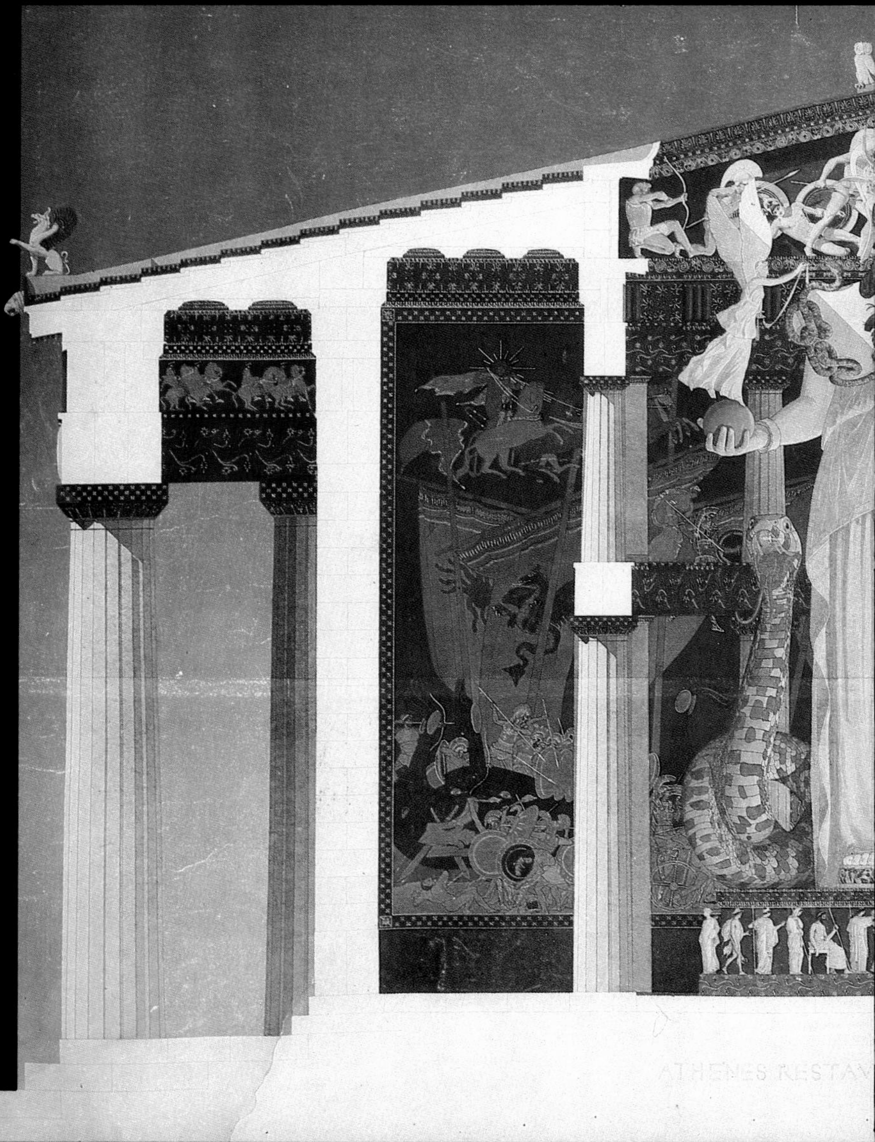
ATHENES

ON DV PARTHENON

by making rich donations to the great panhellenic sanctuaries and building new and more elaborate temples. It was by their gods that they were defined as a people, and their religious practices gave their society a firm structure.

Already in the 6th century the tyrant Peisistratus had recognized the importance of promoting the cults of the gods most beloved by the people of Athens: Demeter, Persephone, Dionysus, and, above all, the city's patron goddess, Athena. He commissioned new buildings on the Acropolis and enhanced the annual festival of the Panathenaea to include athletic and musical contests.

He and his followers also expanded the precinct sacred to Demeter and Persephone at Eleusis, just west of Athens, and fostered the celebration of the mysteries there. During the Persian Wars the complex was burned, but shortly afterward the nobleman Cimon (c. 510–c. 451 BC), a dominant figure in Athens, rebuilt the initiation hall, and Pericles soon doubled its size.

A new temple consecrated to Dionysus was erected on the slope of the Acropolis, and a number of festivals were celebrated in his honor. The most elaborate of these, the Great Dionysia, was marked by contests in poetry and music that ultimately evolved into the classical form of Greek tragedy.

A New Mysticism

In its worship of its civic gods, Athens had clearly not forgotten its origins in the Mycenaean period, when the most important deities were the goddesses of nature,

Another Phidias statue of Athena, the so-called Varvakeion Athena (left), was discovered in Athens in 1881. The satyr opposite cavorts at a Dionysian orgy.

who saw to its annual renewal. Like Demeter and Persephone, Athena was a goddess of fertility and patroness of agriculture who guaranteed the plenty and stability that allowed the community to thrive. By extension, she was seen as the goddess of civic order and peace, one who encouraged the arts by which the state was strengthened.

In time, however, these rather straightforward forms of agrarian mysticism and civic piety failed to satisfy the desire of increasing numbers of people for more direct communication with the supernatural. At the same time that the early philosophers were expounding a new rationalism—undermining the

At the heart of the sanctuary at Eleusis stood the Telesterion, or initiation hall, in which new members were introduced to the mysteries of Demeter and Persephone. It was an extremely large hall supported by pillars, somewhat reminiscent of Persian palaces. After participating in the liturgies performed here, initiates could look forward to a blissful afterlife in the company of the two goddesses who were so generous to mortals.

force of traditional myths—a more violent, frenzied mysticism made its appearance, and with it new gods. Adonis, a Phoenician nature god hitherto unknown in Greece, was fully at home in Athens by about 415 BC. With his gruesome death and joyous resurrection, the handsome youth symbolized the powerful mystery of nature's withering in winter and renewal in spring—both were occasions for ecstatic celebration. Adonis was a favorite of Aphrodite, goddess of love, and the majority of his worshipers were women.

The archetypal healer Asclepius restoring a young woman to health was among the favorite subjects of Greek artists. Healing was held to be a sacred science, and Greek physicians laid the foundations for much of modern medicine.

From the Rational to the Irrational

The cult of Adonis was the first manifestation in Greece of a noisy and emotive Eastern mysticism, one in which the faithful sought to experience in themselves the passion of the god. In the upheaval of the Peloponnesian War, some of this same enthusiasm was accorded to various gods of the classical pantheon, who thus enjoyed a new popularity. A similar frenzy came to accompany the worship of Dionysus, for example. Inflamed by wine, groups of his female followers, called maenads or bacchantes, celebrated his festivals with crazed singing and dancing, expressing frantic grief over the death of the god and joyous abandon over his resurrection. Another deity associated with erotic love was Aphrodite, and she too became the object of more animated worship. In one of her aspects she became a goddess of prostitution, which was avidly practiced in her temple. Asclepius, the god of healing, likewise enjoyed a tremendous upsurge in popularity, and his sanctuary at Epidaurus came to attract more worshipers than any other in all of Greece.

This new intensity in the worship of the traditional gods still failed to satisfy the religious fervor of the age. Soon groups of worshipers were erecting shrines to all manner of foreign gods, most of them from the East. This trend was most apparent in the 3rd and 2nd centuries BC—the early Hellenistic period—and also made itself felt in Rome. But even in its beginnings it marks a profound transformation in Greek religious thinking and experience.

The century of Aristotle—philosopher of reason and patient analyst of the natural world—thus witnessed a first fervent yearning for the supernatural. The irrational was triumphant, as believers in the newer cults willingly surrendered

The cult of Dionysus, god of wine, fertility, and joyous living, was central to Greek religious thinking. Around rustic altars where a statue of the god was driven into the ground, female worshipers, called bacchantes, danced themselves into a frenzy (below and bottom). The ecstatic, even orgiastic

features of the cult were a later development, as the following of the god, mentioned in early Mycenaean-period tablets, was continually enlarged.

themselves
to it. New key
words made their
appearance in the
religious vocabulary:
love, salvation, purification,
and redemption. People responded
to the call of the irrational according to their own
natures; Plato and Praxiteles created radiant worlds
above the one we know, while the poor and uneducated
had to make do with the transport they could find by
joining swooning crowds of intoxicated worshipers.

Philip II of Macedon: New Master of the Age

The upsurge in religious feeling brought with it a degree
of universality that transcended the confines of the city-
state. In some ways this was a welcome development, but
even so it represented yet another blow to the classical
political system, which no longer seemed suited to the
needs of the time. One sure sign of the weakening of
the city-state was the conquest of Greece by Philip II
of Macedon (ruled 359–336 BC). His final victory in
338 BC over the Thebans, Athenians, and their allies
at Chaeronea, in Boeotia, brought to an end the
Greece composed of separate, autonomous states.

The triumphant conqueror, though a great
admirer of Athens, showed nothing but
contempt for the city's most sacred
traditions. One of his successors, Demetrius I
(336–283 BC), went so far as to install his
harem in the Parthenon, and it is said that
he received the homage of a thurifer, a priest
bearing incense, who greeted him, in
repudiation of all that the earlier civic religion
had stood for, with the words: "The other
gods are either remote or do not hear us or
do not exist, or they do not pay any
attention to our needs; you, Demetrius,
are here before us, not in a shape of
wood or stone, but truly present."

The Greeks and Ourselves

It would be a mistake to dwell on such blasphemies or other less savory features of the Hellenistic age ushered in by the Macedonian conquest. Even in their most glorious

Poseidon (left) prepares to hurl his trident. In an austere style, an anonymous artist has captured in bronze the strength, balance, and self-control befitting a god.

era the Greeks had distinguished themselves by their misogyny, their humiliating scorn for those whom they chose to call "barbarians," their murder of helots, and their exploitation of slaves.

Greek history does not end with the arrival of Philip of Macedon. His son Alexander the Great gathered up his own subjects and his Greek allies into one vast force for the purpose of conquering their common enemy, the Persian empire. The new era that followed brought great innovations in science, in the arts, and in religion. For three centuries the intellectual heritage of the Greeks would dominate the region—many aspects of their culture spreading even to the interiors of Asia and Egypt. Moreover, one need only look closely at our own language, our political institutions, and our culture to discover to what extent the Greek experience lives on.

At roughly the same time (5th century BC), a painter at Poseidonia in Magna Graecia painted this mystical scene. A diver plunges into the sea (death), but also into life (eternity), where he will rediscover the primordial waters of life. Overleaf: Apollo playing the kithara.

DOCUMENTS

The Exaltation of Beauty, the Greek Ideal: The *Apollo Belvedere*

With his first book, Reflections on the Imitation of Greek Works in Painting and Sculpture *(1755), German classical archaeologist Johann Joachim Winckelmann (1717–68) did much to change Western artistic tastes by rejecting the style of the baroque and focusing instead on the ideal simplicity of the art of the ancient Greeks, which he held to be a model of eternal and immutable beauty. He followed that work with his important* History of Ancient Art *(1764). Winckelmann is considered the founder of the science of archaeology and chief promoter of the Neoclassical movement of the late 18th and early 19th centuries.*

A "Miracle of Art"

Among all the works of antiquity which have escaped destruction the statue of Apollo is the highest ideal of art. The artist has constructed this work entirely on the ideal, and has employed in its structure just so much only of the material as was necessary to carry out his design and render it visible. This Apollo exceeds all other figures of him as much as the Apollo of Homer excels him whom later poets paint. His stature is loftier than that of man, and his attitude speaks of the greatness with which he is filled. An eternal spring, as in the happy fields of Elysium, clothes with the charms of youth the graceful manliness of ripened years, and plays with softness and tenderness about the proud shape of his limbs.... Neither blood-vessels nor sinews heat and stir this body, but a heavenly essence, diffusing itself like a gentle stream, seems to fill the whole contour of the figure. He has pursued the Python, against which he uses his bow for the first time; with vigorous step he has overtaken the monster and slain it. His lofty look, filled with a consciousness of power, seems to rise far above his victory, and to gaze into infinity. Scorn sits upon his lips, and his nostrils are swelling with suppressed anger, which mounts even to the proud forehead; but the peace which floats upon it in blissful calm remains undisturbed, and his eye is full of sweetness as when the Muses gathered around him seeking to embrace him. The Father of the gods in all the images of him which we have remaining, and which art venerates, does not

The *Apollo Belvedere,* a Roman copy of a Greek statue of the late 4th century BC.

approach so nearly the grandeur in which he manifested himself to the understanding of the divine poet, as he does here in the countenance of his son, and the individual beauties of the other deities are here as in the person of Pandora assembled together, a forehead of Jupiter, pregnant with the Goddess of Wisdom, and eyebrows the contractions of which express their will, the grandly arched eyes of the queen of the gods, and a mouth shaped like that whose touch stirred with delight the loved Branchus. The soft hair plays about the divine head as if agitated by a gentle breeze, like the slender waving tendrils of the noble vine; it seems to be anointed with the oil of the gods, and tied by the Graces with pleasing display on the crown of his head. In the presence of this miracle of art I forget all else, and I myself take a lofty position for the purpose of looking upon it in a worthy manner. My breast seems to enlarge and swell with reverence, like the breasts of those who were filled with the spirit of prophecy, and I feel myself transported to Delos and into the Lycaean groves—places which Apollo honored by his presence—for my image seems to receive life and motion, like the beautiful creation of Pygmalion. How is it possible to paint and describe it! Art itself must counsel me, and guide my hand in filling up hereafter the first outlines which I here have sketched. As they who were unable to reach the heads of the divinities which they wished to crown deposited the garlands at the feet of them, so I place at the feet of this image the conception which I have presented of it.

Johann Joachim Winckelmann
The History of Ancient Art, Book XI
translated by G. Henry Lodge, 1968

Religion in Ancient Athens

In his masterwork, The Ancient City *(1885)—a book that had a profound influence on the historical consciousness of the 19th century—French historian Numa-Denis Fustel de Coulanges (1830–89) presents religion as the guiding principle behind the institutions of both family and city. Here is the magnificent passage in which he analyzes the religious experience of the Athenians.*

Rituals and Traditions

The fear of the gods was not a sentiment peculiar to the Roman; it also reigned in the heart of the Greek. These peoples, originally established by religion, and elevated by it, long preserved the marks of their first education. We know the scruples of the Spartan, who never commenced an expedition before the full moon, who was continually sacrificing victims to know whether he ought to fight, and who renounced the best planned and most necessary enterprises because a bad presage frightened him. The Athenian was not less scrupulous. An Athenian army never set out on a campaign before the seventh day of the month, and when a fleet set sail on an expedition, great care was taken to regild the statue of Pallas.

Xenophon declares that the Athenians had more religious festivals than any other Greek people. "How many victims offered to the gods!" says Aristophanes, "how many temples! how many statues! how many sacred processions! At every moment of the year we see religious feasts and crowned victims." The city of Athens and its territory are covered with temples and chapels. Some are for the city worship, others for the tribe and demes, and still others for family worship. Every house is itself a temple, and in every field there is a sacred tomb.

The Athenian whom we picture to ourselves as so inconstant, so capricious, such a free-thinker, has, on the contrary, a singular respect for ancient traditions and ancient rites. His principal religion —that which secures his most fervent devotion—is the worship of ancestors and heroes. He worships the dead and

Apollo seated on a tripod, a device that in antiquity was considered to be a receptacle for the magical forces of the universe.

fears them. One of his laws obliges him to offer them yearly the first fruits of his harvest; another forbids him to pronounce a single word that can call down their anger. Whatever relates to antiquity is sacred to the Athenian. He has old collections, in which are recorded his rites, from which he never departs. If a priest introduces the slightest innovation into the worship, he is punished with death. The strangest rites are observed from age to age. One day in the year the Athenians offer a sacrifice in honor of Ariadne; and because it was said that the beloved of Theseus died in childbirth, they are compelled to imitate the cries and movements of a woman in travail. They celebrate another festival, called Oschophoria, which is a sort of pantomime, representing the return of

Theseus to Attica. They crown the wand of a herald because Theseus's herald crowned his staff. They utter a certain cry which they suppose the herald uttered, and a procession is formed, and each wears the costume that was in fashion in Theseus's time. On another day the Athenians did not fail to boil vegetables in a pot of a certain kind. This was a rite the origin of which was lost in dim antiquity, and of which no one knew the significance, but which was piously renewed each year.

The Athenian, like the Roman, had unlucky days: on these days no marriage took place, no enterprise was begun, no assembly was held, and justice was not administered. The eighteenth and nineteenth day of every month was employed in purifications. The day of the Plynteria—a day unlucky above all—they veiled the statue of the great Athene Polias. On the contrary, on the day of the Panathenaea, the veil of the goddess was carried in grand procession, and all the citizens, without

A procession in front of the Parthenon, in a 19th-century painting.

distinction of age or rank, made up the *cortège*. The Athenian offered sacrifices for the harvests, for the return of rain, and for the return of fair weather; he offered them to cure sickness, and to drive away famine or pestilence....

In [Athens'] streets we meet at every step soothsayers, priests, and interpreters of dreams. The Athenian believes in portents; sneezing, or a ringing in the ears, arrests him in an enterprise. He never goes on shipboard without taking the auspices. Before marrying he does not fail to consult the flight of birds. The assembly of the people disperses as soon as any one declares that there has appeared in the heavens an ill-boding sign. If a sacrifice has been disturbed by the announcement of bad news, it must be recommenced.

The Athenian hardly commences a sentence without first invoking good fortune.... On the speaker's stand the orator prefers to commence with an invocation to the gods and heroes who inhabit the country. The people are led by oracles. The orators, to give their advice more force, repeat, at every moment, "The goddess ordains thus."

Numa-Denis Fustel de Coulanges
The Ancient City
1885

Prayer on the Acropolis

On his first trip to Athens, when he was a young man, French historian and critic Ernest Renan (1823–92) was moved to write a poem. Years later he published it in his Recollections of My Youth *(1883), giving it the title "Prayer Uttered on the Acropolis When I Had Succeeded in Understanding Its Perfect Beauty."*

Ode to a Temple

"Oh! nobility! Oh! true and simple beauty! Goddess, the worship of whom signifies reason and wisdom, thou whose temple is an eternal lesson of conscience and truth, I come late to the threshold of thy mysteries; I bring to the foot of thy altar much remorse. Ere finding thee, I have had to make infinite search. The initiation which

A reconstruction of the Acropolis, in a 19th-century engraving.

thou didst confer by a smile upon the Athenian at his birth I have acquired by force of reflection and long labor.

"I am born, oh goddess of the blue eyes, of barbarian parents, among the good and virtuous Cimmerians who dwell by the shore of a melancholy sea, bristling with rocks ever lashed by the storm. The sun is scarcely known in this country, its flowers are seaweed, marine plants, and the colored shells which are gathered in the recesses of lonely bays. The clouds seem colorless, and even joy is rather sorrowful there; but fountains of fresh water spring out of the rocks, and the eyes of the young girls are like the green fountains in which, with their beds of waving herbs, the sky is mirrored.

"My forefathers, as far as we can trace them, have passed their lives in navigating the distant seas, which thy

A 19th-century engraving of the Parthenon's west facade.

Argonauts knew not. I used to hear as a child the songs which told of voyages to the Pole; I was cradled amid the souvenir of floating ice, of misty seas like milk, of islands peopled with birds which now and again would warble, and which, when they rose in flight, darkened the air.

"Priests of a strange creed, handed down from the Syrians of Palestine, brought me up. These priests were wise and good. They taught me long lessons of Cronos, who created the world, and of his son, who, as they told me, made a journey upon earth. Their temples are thrice as lofty as thine, oh Eurhythmia, and dense like forests. But they are not enduring, and crumble to pieces at the end of five or six hundred years. They are the fantastic creation of barbarians, who vainly imagine that they can succeed without observing the rules which thou hast laid down, oh Reason! Yet these temples pleased me, for I had not then studied thy divine art and God was present to me in them. Hymns were sung there, and among those which I can remember were: 'Hail star of the sea…Queen of those who mourn in this valley of tears….,' or again, 'Mystical rose, tower of ivory, house of gold, star of the morning….' Yes, Goddess, when I recall these hymns of praise my heart melts, and I become almost an apostate….

"The only way of salvation for the world is by returning to thy allegiance…. Firm in my faith, I shall have force to withstand my evil counsellors, my skepticism, which leads me to doubt of the people, my restless spirit which, after truth has been brought to light, impels to go on searching for it, and my fancy which cannot be still even when Reason has pronounced her judgment. Oh Archegetes, ideal which the man of genius embodies in his masterpieces, I would rather be last in thy house than first in any other. Yes, I will cling to the stylobate of thy temple, I will be a stylites on thy columns, my cell shall be upon thy architrave and what is more difficult still, for thy sake I will endeavor to be intolerant and prejudiced. I will love thee alone. I will learn thy tongue, and unlearn all others. I will be unjust for all that concerns not thee; I will be the servant of the least of thy children. I will exalt and flatter the present inhabitants of the earth which thou gavest to Erecthea. I will endeavor to like their very defects; I will endeavor to persuade myself, oh Hippia, that they are descendants of the horsemen who, aloft upon the marble of thy frieze, celebrate without ceasing their glad festival. I will pluck out of my heart every fibre which is not reason and pure art. I will try to love my bodily ills, to find delight in the flush of fever. Help me! Further my resolutions, oh Salutaris! Help, thou who savest!

"Great are the difficulties which I foresee. Inveterate the habits of mind which I shall have to change. Many the delightful recollections which I shall have to pluck out of my heart. I will try, but I am not very confident of my power. Late in life have I known thee, oh perfect beauty. I shall be beset with hesitations and temptation to fall away. A philosophy, perverse no doubt in its teachings, has led me to believe that good and evil, pleasure and pain, the beautiful and the ungainly, reason and folly, fade into another by shades as impalpable as those in a dove's neck. To feel neither absolute love nor absolute hate becomes therefore wisdom. If any one society, philosophy, or religion had possessed absolute truth, this society, philosophy, or religion, would have vanquished all the others and would be the only one now extant. All those who

have hitherto believed themselves to be right were in error, as we see very clearly. Can we without utter presumption believe that the future will not judge us as we have judged the past? Such are the blasphemous ideas suggested to me by my corrupt mind. A literature wholesome in all respects like thine would now be looked upon as wearisome.

"Thou smilest at my simplicity. Yes, weariness. We are corrupt; what is to be done? I will go further, oh orthodox Goddess, and confide to you the inmost depravation of my heart. Reason and common sense are not all satisfying. There is poetry in the frozen Strymon and in the intoxication of the Thracian. The time will come when thy disciples will be regarded as the disciples of *ennui*. The world is greater than thou dost suppose. If thou hadst seen the Polar snows and the mysteries of the austral firmament, thy forehead, oh Goddess, ever so calm, would be less serene; thy head would be larger and would embrace more varied kinds of beauty....

"A vast stream called Oblivion hurries us downward toward a nameless abyss. Thou art the only true God, oh Abyss! the tears of all nations are true tears; the dreams of all wise men comprise a parcel of truth, all things here below are mere symbols and dreams. The Gods pass away like men, and it would not be well for them to be eternal. The faith which we have felt should never be a chain, and our obligations to it are fully discharged when we have carefully enveloped it in the purple shroud within the folds of which slumber the Gods that are dead."

Ernest Renan
Recollections of My Youth
translated by C. B. Pitman, 1883

The Syllabic Scripts of the Bronze Age Palaces

In the early part of the 2nd millennium BC, on Crete and in mainland Greece, several complex writing systems were devised. Two of the most important ones were the Cretans' Linear A and the Achaeans' Linear B—the second developing from the first.

An Unsolved Mystery

The Cretans developed three successive systems of writing, the first two employing hieroglyphs, the last, Linear A, consisting of patterns of lines. None of these has been deciphered, although the linear script is beginning to disclose some of its secrets. We do not even know what language it denoted. Scholars have suggested everything from some Semitic tongue to proto–Indo-European, the most archaic of languages.

Linear B was devised on the basis of Linear A at an early date, possibly as early as the 17th century BC. It served as the script of the Mycenaean palaces, including those on Crete after the island had been conquered by Achaeans from the mainland. It consists of eighty-eight signs, most of which were borrowed from Linear A. It was finally deciphered by British scholars in 1952, in one of the most fruitful breakthroughs of that period. We now know that the language it reflected was an extremely early form of Greek, older by more than half a millennium than that of the Homeric

L inear A (above) has still not been deciphered. The secrets of Linear B (below) were unlocked by British scholars in 1952.

epics—which helps to confirm the hypothesis that the first Greek-speaking peoples migrated into the region of the Aegean around 2000 BC. Greek is thus one of the oldest documented Indo-European languages. The tablets that have been deciphered provide a wealth of information, often difficult to interpret, relating to the economy of the period: the partition of land, the maintenance of royal herds of cattle, dependence on slaves, etc. The names of the gods also appear with frequency, especially whenever specific vases, incense, or perfumed oils needed to be taken from the royal treasury for specific religious rituals.

The scripts seem to have been used mainly for recordkeeping. In the same period, much more refined consonantal alphabets were being developed in Asia, registering the sounds of individual letters rather than whole syllables. It was from these that the Greek alphabet was derived in the period of the formation of the city-states, opening a new era in the evolution of Greek culture.

Pierre Lévêque

The Pantheon as Reflected in Mycenaean Tablets

Nearly all of the major Olympian gods are mentioned in inscriptions written in Linear B, and it is apparent that many of their names were derived from common nouns. The name Athena, for example, first appears as Potnia *(the mistress); Demeter, as* Matere Teija *(the Divine Mother). Some of the early gods survived as minor deities in the later pantheon, such as Ilithyia, the goddess of childbirth. Others became only attributes of major deities, as is the case with Paiawon (or Paean), who became an epithet of Apollo. Still others disappeared altogether.*

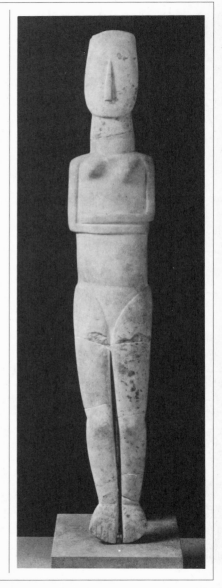

Idols made of every material represent the elemental forces of nature. Opposite: A marble figure from the Cyclades. Left: Bronze and clay statues from Crete.

	GODS	GODDESSES
The Major Olympians	Apollo Ares Dionysus Hades Hephaestus Hermes Poseidon	Aphrodite Artemis Athena Demeter Hera
Early Gods and Goddesses Who Survived Only in Reduced Form	Enyalios Paiawon Smintheus Zagreus	Ephimedeia Erinys Ilithyia Sito
Names of Gods and Goddesses Formed from Common Nouns	Dopota (*dopota*=master) Wanax (*wanax*=king)	Matere Teija (*matere teija*= Divine Mother) Potnia (*potnia*=mistress) Wanasoi (*wanasoi*=queen)

The Evolution of Attic Pottery

The works of Athenian potters reveal distinct and rapid changes in style. The abstraction of the Geometric style of the 8th century BC was followed by a highly decorative Oriental phase. Beginning in the 6th century BC, representations of the human figure became the chief decoration. First came black-figured vases, with the motifs painted in black on the red clay. Then, in 540 BC, this technique was reversed, and the background was painted black while the motifs were left in red. This so-called red-figured technique permitted an incomparable finesse and delicacy of design.

Three distinct pottery styles: A Geometric amphora from the 13th century BC; the celebrated François Vase, c. 570 BC, in the black-figured style; and a red-figured hydria (water jar) created in one of the Greek colonies in southern Italy around 410 BC.

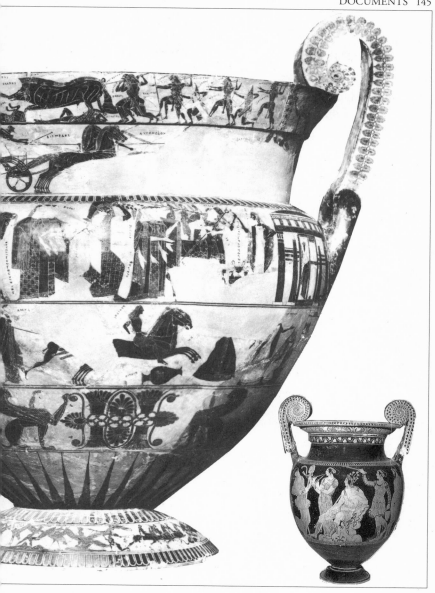

Solon, Legislator and Poet

Solon (c. 630–c. 560 BC) gave the Athenians a new constitution, and at the same time attempted to resolve a tremendous social crisis by canceling the debts of the impoverished farmers. In his elegies he related his actions and promoted his moderate views. Two centuries later, Aristotle included fragments of Solon's poems in his Constitution of Athens.

Aristotle on Solon

That this was the position of affairs all without exception agree, and he himself in his poetry refers to it in the following words:

"For to the people I gave such privilege as suffices,
Neither taking away from or aiming at honour.
But such as possessed power, and from their wealth were leaders,
Them I counselled to retain nothing unseemly.
I stood with my mighty shield thrown around both,
And suffered not either to triumph unrighteously."

And again when expressing his opinion as to how the people ought to be treated:

"The people in this way would follow best with its leaders
Under neither too slack nor too strait a control.
For satiety is the parent of insolence, whenever great prosperity follows
Men whose disposition is not well ordered."…

And again also about the distress of the poor, and those who were before in bondage, but were made free by the cancelling of debts:

"But for what reason I the people whirling
On the axle.…
She best would bear witness in Time's justice,
Mightiest mother of Olympian gods,
Black Earth, whose boundaries fixed

Solon, in a 19th-century engraving based on an Athenian coin.

In many places I formerly plucked up,
She who was before in bondage, but
  now is free.
And I brought back to Athens, to their
  god-founded
Fatherland, many who had been sold,
  one unjustly,
Another justly, and the poor who from
  necessity
Were exiles, no longer giving utterance to
The Attic tongue, in many directions
  wandering about;
Those who on this very spot were
  suffering
Unseemly bondage, trembling at the
  ways of their masters,
Free I set. This too by the strength
Of law, fitting might and right
  together.
I wrought and went through with it
  as I promised.
And laws equally for the good man
  and the bad,
To each fitting straight justice,
I drew up. Another taking the goad
  as I did,
An evil-minded and wealth-loving
  man,
Would not have controlled the people.
  For if I had wished
What pleased my enemies at that
  time....
Of many men would this city have
  been widowed.
For these reasons, girding myself with
  strength on all sides,
I bore me as a wolf amid many
  hounds."

Aristotle
Constitution of Athens
translated by Thomas J. Dymes
1891

Naucratis: A Greek Concession on Egyptian Soil

*In addition to their colonies —which were genuine independent city-states—the Greeks established a number of outposts in foreign territories for the sole purpose of engaging in trade. These markets (*emporia*) were authorized by the local rulers, who stood to profit from regular commerce with the Greeks. One such outpost was at Naucratis, located on the Nile River about midway between modern Cairo and Alexandria. The well-traveled Greek historian Herodotus (5th century BC) describes the relationship between Egypt and the Greek traders.*

Moreover Amasis [Egyptian king Ahmose II (reigned 570–526 BC)] became a lover of the Hellenes; and besides other proofs of friendship which he gave to several among them, he also granted the city of Naucratis for those of them who came to Egypt to dwell in; and to those who did not desire to stay, but who made voyages thither, he granted portions of land to set up altars and make sacred enclosures for their gods. Their greatest enclosure and that one which has most name and is most frequented is called the Hellenion, and this was established by the following cities in common:—of the Ionians

0   100 meters

N →

1   Temple of Aphrodite
2   Temple of Hera
3   Temple of Apollo
4   Temple of the Dioscuri
5   Hellenion

Chios, Teos, Phocaia, Clazomenai, of the Dorians Rhodes, Cnidos, Halicarnassos, Phaselis, and of the Aiolians Mytilene alone. To these belongs this enclosure and these are the cities which appoint superintendents of the port; and all other cities which claim a share in it, are making a claim without any right. Besides this the Eginetans established on their own account a sacred enclosure dedicated to Zeus, the Samians one to Hera, and the Milesians one to Apollo....

Now in old times Naucratis alone was an open trading-place, and no other place in Egypt: and if any one came to any other of the Nile mouths, he was compelled to swear that he came not thither of his own will, and when he had thus sworn his innocence he had to sail with his ship to the Canobic mouth, or if it were not possible to sail by reason of contrary winds, then he had to carry his cargo round the head of the Delta in boats to Naucratis: thus highly was Naucratis privileged.

The History of Herodotus, Book II translated by G. C. Macaulay, 1890

Naucratis, whose temples and network of alleyways have been excavated, was one of the most active trading posts in the Greek world.

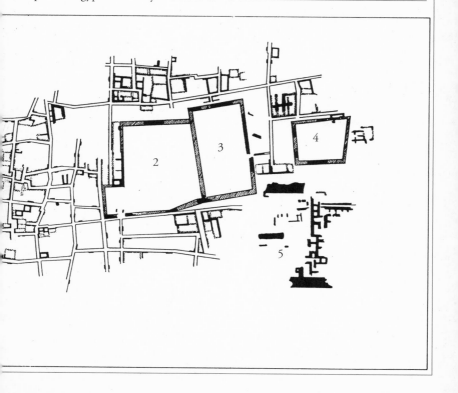

Two Great Pre-Socratic Philosophers from the Beginning of the 5th Century BC

Following the example of his predecessors from Miletus, Heracleitus (c. 540–c. 480 BC) sought the single element that created and brought life to the universe and determined it to be fire. He also believed that the only permanent reality was that of change. Contrarily, Parmenides (born c. 515 BC), founder of the Eleatic School, believed that all perceived change was a sensory illusion.

Diogenes Laertius was a 3rd-century AD Greek biographer. His ten-volume work on the lives of Greek philosophers is the chief source of much of what we now know about these great thinkers.

[Heracleitus] was exceptional from his boyhood; for when a youth he used to say that he knew nothing, although when he was grown up he claimed that he knew everything. He was nobody's pupil, but he declared that he "inquired of himself," and learned everything from himself. Some, however, had said that he had been a pupil of Xenophanes, as we learn from Sotion, who also tells us that Ariston in his book *On Heraclitus* declares that he was cured of the dropsy and died of another disease. And Hippobotus has the same story.

As to the work which passes as his, it is a continuous treatise *On Nature*, but is divided into three discourses, one on the universe, another on politics, and a third on theology. This book he deposited in the temple of Artemis and, according to some, he deliberately made it the more obscure in order that none but adepts should approach it, and lest familiarity should breed contempt. Of our philosopher Timon gives a sketch in these words:

"In their midst uprose shrill, cuckoo-like, a mob-reviler, riddling Heraclitus."

Theophrastus puts it down to melancholy that some parts of his work are half-finished, while other parts make a strange medley. As a proof of his magnanimity, Antisthenes in his *Successions of Philosophers* cites the fact that he renounced his claim to the kingship in favour of his brother. So great fame did his book win that a sect was founded and called the Heracliteans, after him.

Greek poetry was intimately associated with music. Here the legendary poet Linus and his pupil Iphicles are depicted on a 5th-century BC vase.

Here is a general summary of his doctrines. All things are composed of fire, and into fire they are again resolved; further, all things come about by destiny, and existent things are brought into harmony by the clash of opposing currents; again, all things are filled with souls and divinities. He has also given an account of all the orderly happenings in the universe, and declares the sun to be no larger than it appears. Another of his sayings is: "Of soul thou shalt never find boundaries, not if thou trackest it on every path; so deep is its cause." Self-conceit he used to call a falling sickness (epilepsy) and eyesight a lying sense. Sometimes, however, his utterances are clear and distinct, so that even the

dullest can easily understand and derive therefrom elevation of soul. For brevity and weightiness his exposition is incomparable.

Coming now to his particular tenets, we may state them as follows: fire is the element, all things are exchanged for fire and come into being by rarefaction and condensation; but of this he gives no clear explanation. All things come into being by conflict of opposites, and the sum of things flows like a stream. Further, all that is limited and forms one world. And it is alternately born from fire and again resolved into fire in fixed cycles to all eternity, and this is determined by destiny. Of the opposites that which tends to birth or creation is called war and strife, and that which

An engraving of the Ephesian philosopher Heracleitus.

HERACLITE Philosophe
Ephesien dit le Tenebreux il tenoit le
Feu pour principe de toutes choses il pleuroit
amerement les miseres des hommes, mourut
d'hidropisie agé de 60 ans.

tends to destruction by fire is called concord and peace. Change he called a pathway up and down, and this determines the birth of the world.

For fire by contracting turns into moisture, and this condensing turns into water; water again when congealed turns into earth. This process he calls the downward path. Then again earth is liquefied, and thus gives rise to water, and from water the rest of the series is derived. He reduces nearly everything to exhalation from the sea. This process is the upward path. Exhalations arise from earth as well as from sea; those from sea are bright and pure, those from earth dark. Fire is fed by the bright exhalations, the moist element by the others. He does not make clear the nature of the surrounding element. He says, however, that there are in it bowls with their concavities turned towards us, in which the bright exhalations collect and produce flames. These are the stars. The flame of the sun is the brightest and the hottest; the other stars are further from the earth and for that reason give it less light and heat. The moon, which is nearer to the earth, traverses a region which is not pure. The sun, however, moves in a clear and untroubled region, and keeps a proportionate distance from us. That is why it gives us more heat and light. Eclipses of the sun and moon occur when the bowls are turned upwards; the monthly phases of the moon are due to the bowl turning round in its place little by little. Day and night, months, seasons and years, rains and winds and other similar phenomena are accounted for by the various exhalations.

Diogenes Laertius
Lives of Eminent Philosophers
translated by R. D. Hicks, 1925

Only fragments of Parmenides' work have survived. Here is the first part of his poem On Nature, *in which he sets forth his beliefs.*

FRAGMENT I

The mares that carry me, as far as
  impulse might reach,
Were taking me, when they brought
  and placed me upon the much-
  speaking route
Of the goddess, that carries everywhere
  unscathed the man who knows;
Thereon was I carried, for thereon the
  much-guided mares were carrying me,
Straining to pull the chariot, and
  maidens were leading the way.
The axle, glowing in its naves, gave
  forth the shrill sound of a pipe,
(For it was urged on by two rounded
Wheels at either end), even while
  maidens, Daughters of the Sun,
  were hastening
To escort me, after leaving the House
  of Night for the light,
Having pushed back with their hands
  the veils from their heads.
There are the gates of the paths
  of Night and Day,
And a lintel and a threshold of stone

surround them,
And the aetherial gates themselves
  are filled with great doors;
And for these Justice, much-avenging,
  holds the keys of retribution.
Coaxing her with gentle words,
  the maidens
Did cunningly persuade her that
  she should push back the bolted
  bar for them
Swiftly from the gates; and these made
  of the doors
A gaping gap as they were opened wide,
Swinging in turn in their sockets the
  brazen posts
Fitted with rivets and pins; straight
  through them at that point
Did the maidens drive the chariot and
  mares along the broad way.
And the goddess received me
  kindly, and took my right hand
  with her hand,
And uttered speech and thus
  addressed me:
"Youth attended by immortal
  charioteers,
Who come to our House with mares
  that carry you,
Welcome; for it is no ill fortune that
  sent you forth to travel
This route (for it lies far indeed from
  the beaten track of men),
But right and justice. And it is right
  that you should learn all things,
Both the steadfast heart of
  persuasive truth,
And the beliefs of mortals, in which
  there is no true trust.
But nevertheless you shall learn
  these things as well, how the things
  which seem
Had to have genuine existence,
  permeating all things completely."
Parmenides of Elea: Fragments
translated by David Gallop, 1984

Democrats and Democratic Regimes of the 6th and 5th Centuries BC

Tyrants, reformers, and other sorts of leaders all contributed to the gradual establishment of democracy in Athens. Presented here are portraits of three men who played a vital role in the process: Peisistratus (c. 605–527 BC), Cleisthenes (c. 570–c. 507 BC), and Pericles (c. 495–429 BC).

This description of Peisistratus's rule is taken from an account of the government of Athens written by Aristotle in the 4th century BC.

The tyranny of Peisistratus was at first established in this way, and experienced the changes just enumerated. As we have said, Peisistratus administered the government with moderation, and more like a citizen than a tyrant. For, in applying the laws, he was humane and mild, and towards offenders clement, and, further, he used to advance money to the needy for their agricultural operations, thus enabling them to carry on the cultivation of their lands uninterruptedly. And this he did with two objects: that they might not live in the city, but being scattered over the country, and enjoying moderate means and engaged in their own affairs, they might have neither the desire nor the leisure to concern themselves with public matters. At the same time he had the advantage of a greater revenue from the careful cultivation of the land; for he took a tithe of the produce.

It was for this reason, too, that he instituted jurors throughout the demes, and often, leaving the capital, made tours in the country, seeing matters for himself, and reconciling such as had differences, so that they might have no occasion to come to the city and neglect their lands.

It was on such a tour that the incident is said to have occurred about the man in Hymettus, who was cultivating what was afterwards called

the "No-Tax-Land." For seeing a man delving at rocks with a wooden peg and working away, he wondered at his using such a tool, and bade his attendants ask what the spot produced. "Every ill and every woe under the sun," replied the man, "and Peisistratus must take his tithe of these ills and these woes." Now, the man made this answer not knowing who he was; but Peisistratus, pleased at his boldness of speech and love of work, gave him immunity from all taxes. And he never interfered with the people in any other way indeed during his rule, but ever cultivated peace and watched over it in times of tranquillity. And this is the reason why it often passed as a proverb that the tyranny of Peisistratus was the life of the Golden Age; for it came to pass afterwards, through the insolence of his sons, that the government became much harsher. But what more than any other of his qualities made him a favourite was his popular sympathies and kindness of disposition. For while in all other matters it was his custom to govern entirely according to the laws, so he never allowed himself any unfair advantage.

Aristotle
Constitution of Athens
translated by Thomas J. Dymes, 1891

Herodotus's History, *written in the 5th century BC, is mainly about Greece's wars with Persia, but—to our great benefit— there are many often-lengthy digressions.*

Athens, which even before that time was great, then, after having been freed from despots, became gradually yet greater; and in it two men exercised power, namely Cleisthenes a descendant of Alcmaion, the same who is reported to have bribed the Pythian prophetess, and Isagoras the son of Tisander, of a family which was highly reputed, but his original descent I am not able to declare; his kinsmen however offer sacrifices to the Carian Zeus. These men came to party strife for power; and when Cleisthenes was being worsted in the struggle, he made common cause with the people.

After this he caused the Athenians to be in ten tribes, who were formerly in four; and he changed the names by which they were formerly called after the sons of Ion, namely Geleon, Aigicoreus, Argades, and Hoples, and invented for them names taken from other heroes, all native Athenians except Ajax, whom he added as a neighbour and ally, although he was no Athenian....

Thus had the Cleisthenes of Sikyon done: and the Athenian Cleisthenes, who was his daughter's son and was called after him, despising, as I suppose, the Ionians, as he the Dorians, imitated his namesake Cleisthenes in order that the Athenians might not have the same tribes as the Ionians: for when at the time of which we speak he added to his own party the whole body of the common people of the Athenians, which in former time he had despised, he changed the names of the tribes and made them more in number than they had been; he made in fact ten rulers of

tribes instead of four, and by tens also he distributed the demes in the tribes; and having added the common people to his party he was much superior to his opponents.

The History of Herodotus, Book V
translated by G. C. Macaulay, 1890

Thucydides' only work, a chronicle of the Peloponnesian War, includes detailed analyses of the thoughts and actions of key participants in the conflict.

By these and similar words Pericles endeavoured to appease the anger of the Athenians against himself, and to divert their minds from their terrible situation. In the conduct of public affairs they took his advice, and sent no more embassies to Sparta; they were again eager to prosecute the war. Yet in private they felt their sufferings keenly; the common people had been deprived even of the little which they possessed, while the upper class had lost fair estates in the country with all their houses and rich furniture.

Worst of all, instead of enjoying peace, they were now at war. The popular indignation was not pacified until they had fined Pericles; but soon afterwards, with the usual fickleness of a multitude, they elected him general and committed all their affairs to his charge. Their private sorrows were beginning to be less acutely felt, and for a time of public need they thought that there was no man like him.

During the peace while he was at the head of affairs he ruled with prudence; under his guidance Athens was safe, and reached the height of her greatness in his time. When the war began he showed that here too he had formed a true estimate of the Athenian power.

Pericles speaking to the people of Athens.

He survived the commencement of hostilities two years and six months; and, after his death, his foresight was even better appreciated than during his life. For he had told the Athenians that if they would be patient and would attend to their navy, and not seek to enlarge their dominion while the war was going on, nor imperil the existence of the city, they would be victorious; but they did all that he told them not to do, and in matters which seemingly had

nothing to do with the war, from motives of private ambition and private interest they adopted a policy which had disastrous effects in respect both of themselves and of their allies; their measures, had they been successful, would only have brought honour and profit to individuals, and, when unsuccessful, crippled the city in the conduct of the war.

The reason of the difference was that he, deriving authority from his capacity and acknowledged worth, being also a man of transparent integrity, was able to control the multitude in a free spirit; he led them rather than was led by them; for, not seeking power by dishonest arts, he had no need to say pleasant things, but, on the strength of his own high character, could venture to oppose and even to anger them. When he saw them unseasonably elated and arrogant, his words humbled and awed them; and, when they were depressed by groundless fears, he sought to reanimate their confidence. Thus Athens, though still in name a democracy, was in fact ruled by her greatest citizen.

Thucydides, Book II
translated by Benjamin Jowett, 1900

An Opponent of Athenian Democracy: Pseudo-Xenophon, the "Old Oligarch"

We are fortunate in possessing an anonymous text—once falsely attributed to Greek historian Xenophon (c. 431–c. 352 BC)—entitled The Constitution of the Athenians, *by the "Old Oligarch." Staunchly loyal to the aristocracy, its author paints a very lucid picture of the political scene of his time, clearly showing that in his opinion the people, whom he calls the evil ones, are right in acting as they do.*

Indeed, as to the constitution of the Athenians my opinion is that I do not at all approve of their having chosen this form of constitution because by making this choice they have given the advantages to the vulgar people at the cost of the good. This is the reason for my disapproval.…

In the first place I now want to say that there it seems just that the vulgar, the poor and the people are given the preference to the distinguished and rich people, for the simple reason that the people is the motive power in the navy and gives the state its strength.…

This now being the case, it seems fully justified that everybody is admitted to the offices, both by the lot-drawing now in force and by the other elections, and that any of the citizens wishing it may be allowed to speak.

A 19th-century engraving depicting figures from the Homeric epics.

Then there are the offices of benefit to the whole people when well conducted, but which in the opposite case mean a danger; these offices the people do not feel inclined to be admitted to at all....

For the people acknowledge that it is more useful for themselves not to hold these offices, but to leave them to the best qualified men. But all the offices where it is a question of receiving fees and of deriving personal advantage, those the people try to be admitted to.

Then there is the thing at which several people wonder, that they everywhere give the vulgar and the poor and the common people the preference to the aristocrats, but it will be seen that exactly by this means they back up the democracy. For when the poor, the people of small means,

and the low individuals are prospering and their number is increasing, they will strengthen the democracy. If, on the contrary, the rich and distinguished people are prospering, the proletarians are strengthening their opposites.

For in every country the aristocracy is contrasted to the democracy, there being in the best people the least licentiousness and iniquity, but the keenest eyes for morals; in the people on the other hand we find a very high degree of ignorance, disorder, and vileness; for poverty more and more leads them in the direction of bad morals, thus also the absence of education and in the case of some persons the ignorance which is due to the want of money.

Anonymous
The Constitution of the Athenians
translated by Hartvig Frisch, 1952

An Orgiastic Cult: Maenadism

Ancient Greece was once aptly characterized as having been divided between an Apollonian and a Dionysian spirit—the one serene and controlled, the other ecstatic and unbridled. The latter is best exemplified in the ravings of the bacchantes, or maenads (literally, madwomen). These ardent worshipers of Dionysus were frequently portrayed on ancient vases and immortalized by 5th-century BC playwright Euripides in his tragedy The Bacchae.

The Double Nature of Dionysus

In ancient Greece, it was the women whose lives were traditionally most confined who became [Dionysus's] most enthusiastic worshipers. The god "pricks them to leave their looms and shuttles." Again and again in the god's myths we come across Argive women, Rhodian women, Athenian women, ripped loose from the humdrum, orderly activities of their domestic lives and, intoxicated by the god, being transformed into enraptured, manic dancers in the wilderness of the mountains.... Once again, we are confronted with the god's double nature: the bringer of liberation, ecstasy, inspiration and the most blessed deliverance is also the bringer of madness, violence, wildness, terror. He is known as "the roarer," "the loud-shouter," "the ear-splitter," but he is just as powerfully revealed in the fathomless silence as in the pandemonium that he stirs up. He appears as a bull, a bear, a lion, a panther, but he also transforms himself into a young girl, a tree, flowing water. The numinous feeling that he inspires shatters all order and composure and can lead either to the ecstatic experience of the divine or to hysteria and bloodthirsty destructiveness.

Arianna Huffington
The Gods of Greece, 1993

From *The Bacchae*

His mother first, being high priestess,
  now began the kill,
and rushed at him....
Caressing her cheek he said,
  "Mother, it's I,

A late 5th-century BC krater decorated with figures of swooning maenads.

A 19th-century portrayal of a bacchanal.

Pentheus, your own child, I whom
  you bore
to Echion. Oh Mother, take pity on me—
do not, for the wrongs I've done, kill
  your own child!"
But she, spitting foam, rolling her eyes
  convulsed,
gone out of her right mind, was in
  the grip
of ecstasy, not listening to him.
She took hold of his left arm by the hand,
and, her foot braced upon the poor
  man's ribs,
wrenched out the shoulder, not by her
  own strength,
but on her hands the god conferred
  such ease.
Ino was finishing off the other side,
breaking his flesh, and Autonoë,
  the whole pack
of Bacchae were at him.

A general howl arose,
he groaning as long as there was breath
  in him
and the women yelling victory, as one
carried off an arm, another carried
  his feet
still in their boots. His ribs were laid
  quite bare
in the dismemberment. With bloodied
  hands
each woman played ball with scraps of
  Pentheus' flesh.

His body lies dispersed, one part below
the rugged cliffs, another among the
  leafage
of the deep woods, no easy thing to find.
His mother somehow got into her hands
his battered head, and stuck it on
  the point
of her thyrsus, just as if she were carrying
down from Cithairon's crags a lion's head.
                                Euripides
                                The Bacchae
          translated by Donald Sutherland, 1968

A Stirring Appeal for Patriotism

In his first "Philippic," an oration delivered in 351 BC, Athenian statesman Demosthenes (384–322 BC) attempted with all the eloquence at his command to convince the people of Athens to take action against Philip II of Macedon. He presented two possible policies: cowardly inaction, the catastrophic results of which were obvious, or courage, which might rouse the entire city-state against the scandalous designs of the king of Macedon, enabling citizen-soldiers to be sent against his forces instead of indifferent foreign mercenaries. The oration is possibly the finest of those of Demosthenes to survive; however, from the fact that the situation with respect to Philip remained unchanged in the following years, it is obvious that it had little effect.

"Attend to Your Duty"

By 351 BC, Philip II's plan for the expansion of the kingdom of Macedon was well underway. Demosthenes perceived the imminence of the threat to Athens and delivered the first of a series of three "Philippics"— spirited denunciations against the city's archenemy. Demosthenes was a model of patriotism, as intelligent as he was resolute. When Athens was decisively defeated by Philip's successors, he committed suicide rather than submit.

And it seems, men of Athens, as if some god, ashamed for us at our proceedings, has put this activity into Philip. For had he been willing to remain quiet in possession of his conquests and prizes, and attempted nothing further, some of you, I think, would be satisfied with a state of things, which brands our nation with the shame of cowardice and the foulest disgrace. But by continually encroaching and grasping after more, he may possibly rouse you, if you have not altogether despaired. I marvel,

Coins minted by Philip II of Macedon, the archenemy of Athens (above and opposite).

indeed, that none of you, Athenians, notices with concern and anger, that the beginning of this war was to chastise Philip, the end is to protect ourselves against his attacks. One thing is clear: he will not stop, unless some one oppose him. And shall we wait for this? And if you despatch empty galleys and hopes from this or that person, think ye all is well? Shall we not embark? Shall we not sail with at least a part of our national forces, now though not before? Shall we not make a descent upon his coast? Where, then, shall we land? some one asks. The war itself, men of Athens, will discover the rotten parts of his empire, if we make a trial; but if we sit at home, hearing the orators accuse and malign one another, no good can ever be achieved. Methinks, where a portion of our citizens, though not all, are commissioned with the rest, Heaven blesses, and Fortune aids the struggle: but where you send out a general and an empty decree and hopes from the hustings, nothing that you desire is done; your enemies scoff, and your allies die for fear of such an armament. For it is impossible—aye, impossible, for one man to execute all your wishes: to promise, and assert, and accuse this or that person, is possible; but so your affairs are ruined. The general commands wretched unpaid hirelings; here are persons easily found, who tell you lies of his conduct; you vote at random from what you hear: what then can be expected?

How is this to cease, Athenians? When you make the same persons soldiers, and witnesses of the general's conduct, and judges when they return home at his audit; so that you may not only hear of your own affairs, but be present to see them. So disgraceful is our condition now, that every general is twice or thrice tried before you for his life, though none dares even once to hazard his life against the enemy: they prefer the death of kidnappers and

A bust of Demosthenes, who is considered to have been one of ancient Greece's finest orators.

Detail of a 4th-century BC bas-relief commemorating a treaty between Athens and the island of Samos.

thieves to that which becomes them; for it is a malefactor's part to die by sentence of the law, a general's to die in battle. Among ourselves, some go about and say that Philip is concerting with the Lacedaemonians the destruction of Thebes and the dissolution of republics; some, that he has sent envoys to the king; others, that he is fortifying cities in Illyria: so we wander about, each inventing stories. For my part, Athenians, by the gods I believe, that Philip is intoxicated with the magnitude of his exploits, and has many such dreams in his imagination, seeing the absence of opponents, and elated by success; but most certainly he has no such plan of action, as to let the silliest people among us know what his intentions are; for the silliest are these newsmongers.

Let us dismiss such talk, and remember only that Philip is an enemy, who robs us of our own and has long insulted us; that wherever we have expected aid from any quarter, it has been found hostile, and that the future depends on ourselves, and unless we are willing to fight him there, we shall perhaps be compelled to fight here. This let us remember, and then we shall have determined wisely, and have done with idle conjectures. You need not pry into the future, but assure yourselves it will be disastrous, unless you attend to your duty, and are willing to act as becomes you.

Demosthenes,
The Olynthiac and Other Public Orations,
translated by Charles Rann Kennedy,
1910

Ancient Greece
(6000–323 BC)

Neolithic Period 6000–2600 BC	Settlers from Asia Minor bring knowledge of agriculture to indigenous populations of mainland Greece
Early Bronze Age 2600–2000 BC	Establishment of Lerna, a city on the Gulf of Argolis
	c. 2000 BC Arrival on mainland Greece of first Greek-speaking peoples
Middle Bronze Age 2000–1700 BC	**c. 2000–c. 1750 BC** Erection of the first Minoan palaces on Crete; development of the Linear A writing system
Late Bronze Age 1700–1200 BC (**Mycenaean Period**)	**c. 1550 BC** Destruction of the first Minoan palaces and building of the second; development of Linear B
	Construction and enlargement of the Mycenaean palaces
	c. 1500 BC Conquest of Crete by the Achaeans
	c. 1200 BC Trojan War; destruction of the Mycenaean palaces
Dark Ages 1200–c. 800 BC	**c. 1100 BC** Beginning of the Iron Age; development of proto-Geometric style of art
	1100–1000 BC Greek settlements founded on the coast of Asia Minor by Dorians, Ionians, and Aeolians
	1000–850 BC Formation of the Homeric kingdoms
Archaic Period c. 800–500 BC	Birth of the Geometric style; development of a Greek alphabet
	c. 800 BC Formation of city-states; renewed mercantile expansion
	776 BC Founding of the Olympic Games
	c. 750 BC Beginning of colonial expansion
	c. 594 BC Solon elected archon of Athens; institutes economic and constitutional reforms
	c. 507 BC Cleisthenes reforms political organization of Athens
Classical Period 500–300 BC	**500–449 BC** Persian Wars
	478 BC Creation of the Delian League
	c. 470 BC Birth of Socrates
	c. 460 BC Democratic reforms in Athens under Pericles
	447–432 BC Erection of the Parthenon
	431–404 BC Peloponnesian War and decline of Athens
	399 BC Death of Socrates
	384 BC Birth of Aristotle
	371–362 BC Dominance of Thebes
	338 BC Conquest of Greece by Philip II of Macedon
	336–323 BC Reign of Alexander the Great

Further Reading

Aristotle, *Constitution of Athens,* translated by Thomas J. Dymes, Seeley & Co., Ltd., London, 1891

Austin, M. M., and Pierre Vidal-Naquet, *Economic and Social History of Ancient Greece,* University of California Press, Berkeley, 1978

Betancourt, Philip P., *The History of Minoan Pottery,* Princeton University Press, New Jersey, 1985

Beye, Charles R., *Ancient Greek Literature and Society,* Cornell University Press, Ithaca, New York, 1987

Boardman, John, *Greek Art,* Thames and Hudson, New York, 1985

Chadwick, John, *The Decipherment of Linear B,* Cambridge University Press, New York, 1990

Charbonneaux, J., et al., *Classical Greek Art 480–330 BC,* Braziller, New York, 1972

Christopoulos, George A., et al., *History of the Hellenic World: Prehistory and Protohistory to 1100 BC,* Pennsylvania State University Press, University Park, 1974

The Constitution of the Athenians, translated by Hartvig Frisch, Nordisk Forlag, Copenhagen, 1952

Diogenes Laertius, *Lives of Eminent Philosophers,* translated by R. D. Hicks, G. P. Putnam's Sons, New York, 1925

Euripides, *The Bacchae,* translated by Donald Sutherland, University of Nebraska Press, Lincoln, 1968

Farrar, Cynthia, *The Origins of Democratic Thinking: The Invention of Politics in Classical Athens,* Cambridge University Press, New York, 1988

Finley, M. I., *The World of Odysseus,* Peter Smith, Magnolia, Massachusetts, 1988

Forrest, W. G., *The Emergence of Greek Democracy: The Character of Greek Politics, 800–400 BC,* Weidenfeld and Nicolson, London, 1966

Fustel de Coulanges, Numa-Denis, *The Ancient City,* Johns Hopkins University Press, Baltimore, 1980

Graham, James W., et al., *The Palaces of Crete,* Princeton University Press, New Jersey, 1987

Grant, Michael, *The Rise of the Greeks,* Charles Scribner's Sons, New York, 1987

Guthrie, W. K., *Greek Philosophers: From Thales to Aristotle,* HarperCollins, New York, 1960

The History of Herodotus, translated by G. C. Macaulay, Macmillan and Co., New York, 1890

Huffington, Arianna, *The Gods of Greece,* Grove/Atlantic, New York, 1993

Loraux, N., *The Invention of Athens,* translated by A. Sheridan, Harvard University Press, Cambridge, Massachusetts, 1986

Luce, John V., *An Introduction to Greek Philosophy,* Thames and Hudson, New York, 1993

McLellan, Elizabeth, *Minoan Crete,* Longman, White Plains, New York, 1976

Parmenides, *Parmenides of Elea: Fragments,* translated by David Gallop, University of Toronto Press, Canada, 1984

Papaioannou, Kostas, *The Art of Greece,* Abrams, New York, 1988

Renan, Ernest, *Recollections of My Youth,* translated by C. B. Pitman, G. P. Putnam's Sons, New York, 1883

Starr, Chester G., *The Ancient Greeks,* Oxford University Press, New York, 1971

Thucydides, translated by Benjamin Jowett, Clarendon Press, Oxford, 1900

Vidal-Naquet, Pierre, *The Black Hunter: Forms of Thought and Forms of Society in the Greek World,* translated by Andrew Szegedy-Maszak, Johns Hopkins University Press, Baltimore, 1986

List of Illustrations

Index

Photograph Credits

Text Credits

Grateful acknowledgment is made for use of material from the following: *The Bacchae of Euripides*, translated with a critical essay by Donald Sutherland. Reprinted by permission of the University of Nebraska Press. Copyright © 1968 by the University of Nebraska Press (pp. 160–3); *Diogenes Laertius: Lives of Eminent Philosophers*, vol. 2, translated by R. D. Hicks, William Heinemann, London, 1925 (pp. 150–3); Hartvig Frisch, trans. and ed., *The Constitution of the Athenians*, 1942, Politiken Forlag, Copenhagen, Denmark (p. 159); Arianna Huffington, *The Gods of Greece*, copyright © 1993 Arianna Huffington and Françoise Gilot. Used by permission of Grove/Atlantic, Inc. (p. 160); Henry Miller, *The Colossus of Maroussi*. Copyright 1941 by Henry Miller. Reprinted by permission of New Directions Publishing Corp. (inside front cover); *Parmenides of Elea: Fragments*, text and translation by David Gallop, © University of Toronto Press, 1984. Reprinted by permission of University of Toronto Press Incorporated (p. 153); Johann Joachim Winckelmann, *History of Ancient Art*, translated by G. Henry Lodge, 1968. The Crossroad Publishing Company (p. 131)

Pierre Lévêque is a professor of Greek history at the Université de Franche-Comté, in Besançon. In addition to his scholarly histories of Greece, he has published several popular surveys of ancient Greek culture as well as guidebooks to Greece and Sicily. His most recent published works are about the history of religion.

To the memory of Aléka
and of Jenny
and for all Greek friends

Translated from the French by Anthony Zielonka

Project Manager: Sharon AvRutick
Typographic Designer: Elissa Ichiyasu
Editor: Russell M. Stockman
Assistant Editor: Jennifer Stockman
Design Assistants: Penelope Hardy and Miko McGinty
Text Permissions: Neil Ryder Hoos

Library of Congress Catalog Card Number: 93–72816

ISBN 0–8109–2843–4

Copyright © 1990 Gallimard

English translation copyright © 1994 Harry N. Abrams, Inc., New York,
and Thames and Hudson Ltd., London

Published in 1994 by Harry N. Abrams, Incorporated, New York

Printed and bound in Italy by Editoriale Lloyd, Trieste